GOD
IS LOOKING FOR A
Woman

Woman, Thou Art Favored

BETTY SPELLS

iUniverse LLC
Bloomington

GOD IS LOOKING FOR A WOMAN
Woman, Thou Art Favored

iUniverse books may be ordered through booksellers or by contacting:

iUniverse LLC
1663 Liberty Drive
Bloomington, IN 47403
www.iuniverse.com
1-800-Authors (1-800-288-4677)

ISBN: 978-1-4917-1918-3 (sc)
ISBN: 978-1-4917-1960-2 (e)

Library of Congress Control Number: 2013923009

Printed in the United States of America.

iUniverse rev. date: 02/18/2014

CONTENTS

DEDICATION

I dedicate this book to the Godly strong women that have been in my life to shape me and to train me to be the Godly strong woman that I am today. It is dedicated first to Marie Clark Overstreet, a true Proverbs 31 woman and my mother. Also, I would like to dedicate this book to my grandmothers: Marzella Boston Clark, the humblest person that I have ever known and Alice Overstreet Anderson, my most energetic and humorous grandmother. (Both are deceased.) This book is dedicated to my beloved oldest sister Elsie Ree Overstreet Hardy, who recently went home to be with the Lord. She showed and taught me a strong uncompromising love for family. Lastly, I would like to dedicate this book to my sister, Willie Mae Overstreet McElroy, who is also older than I am. She also taught me many things and showed me what it is like to have a best friend growing up in the same house. These women were all about love.

SPECIAL THANKS

First and foremost, I thank God. Then, I would like to especially thank the men and women who have stood with me, encouraged me, helped me and just loved me. Special thanks go to my family; I thank my Dad and Mom, Holly and Marie Overstreet for believing in me and supporting me in all of my endeavors including being members and elders of the church that I pastor. I thank my natural brothers: Hollie Jr., David Louis, Willie, and Michael Overstreet and my sisters: Willie Mae (Katy) McElroy, Rosie Crowell and Lorie Scott for being there for me when I need them. Special thanks to my brothers-in-law, Pastor Frederick Crowell and my assistant, Pastor Lucius Scott for the love and support that they show me as fellow ministers of the Gospel. Last but definitely not least, I thank my two sons, Joel Isaiah Spells and Gabriel Hosea Spells whose lives God gave me the privilege to mold and shape. If I may take just one moment to brag, they are exemplary, extraordinary young men who are the apple of God's eye and certainly mine.

Also, to my many uncles and aunts, nephews and nieces and cousins, thank you. To my dear friends, especially Mrs. Josephine Virgil-Hughes, thank you. To all of my pastors and ministers friends, thank you. I would like to say special thanks to my church family, True Foundation Ministry, the church in which God uses me to Pastor, especially my spiritual sons and daughters that have been with me for 23+ years: Marie Overstreet, Lucius & Lorie Scott and Family, Stancil & Mary Blanks and Family, Otha Brown, Evelyn Brown, Lennette Young and Teresa Presswood. I would like to triple thank the man and woman of God who have covered me in ministry for more than 21 years, Apostle Leonard and Prophetess Varnise Lucas and their church family, Light City Church of New Orleans, Louisana who also is our church family.

BIBLIOGRAPHY

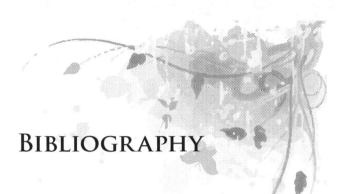

The Holy Bible (King James Version), Camden, NJ: Thomas Nelson Incorporation, 1972.

The Holy Bible (New International Version), Grand Rapids, MI: The Zondervan Corporation, 1996.

The New International Webster's Standard Dictionary (2006 edition.). (2006). USA: Trident

Reference Publishing.

www.experienceproject.com/groups/Am-A-Pastors-Wife/56348

www.engagingchurchblog.com/staggering-statistics-of-unhappy-pastors

www.Maranathalife.com/lifeline/stats.htm

www.Triblive.com/x/pittsburghtrib/news/s_641857.html

AUTOBIOGRAPHY

Betty Diane Overstreet Spells was born December 14, 1957 in a small town called Marion, Mississippi. She is the fifth child of nine born to Holly and Marie Clark Overstreet whom still reside in Marion. She is the middle child among four sisters and four brothers being the core or in the very center. Betty grew up in a rural country setting with a very loving family and an extended family to shape and mold her. She attended Meridian Junior College and Mississippi State University—Meridian Campus and received a Bachelor of Science Degree in Elementary Education K-8. She taught in the public schools settings for fourteen and a half years and in a private school setting for three years. She went back to college at The University of West Alabama and received a Master Degree in Counseling Psychology. In continuing her education, she went to Mississippi State University—Meridian Campus and completed a Specialist Degree in Community Counseling. Presently, she works at a mental health center as a therapist who is a License Practicing Counselor (LPC) and a Nationally Certified Counselor (NCC) serving youths ages 5-18.

Betty whole life has always been centered around the Lord. She loves the Lord with all of her heart. Beginning at an early age, she served the LORD. Betty grew up in the church, and during her childhood and teenage years, she served diligently as a junior usher, secretary, choir member and where ever she could serve or was asked to serve in the church. Later on, she and her husband at that time established a church where she served as co-pastor for nearly twenty years. Then she began to serve as senior pastor at the church that she presently attends. True Foundation Ministry was established in 2009 by Betty and the majority of the members that attend.

Betty has two very intelligent handsome grown-up sons: Joel Isaiah Spells and Gabriel Hosea Spells of whom she is very proud of. She resides in Meridian, MS just across the line from Marion, MS, her home town.

Book Summary

This book was written to remind some and to make others aware that we belong to God, and it is God's right to orchestrate our lives. Men and women were created by God. Since God is the creator, He is the only one that knows what He created us to do and to be. Man should not dictate over others by telling them what they should do; unless, their words are coming directly from God. No one should allow man to manipulate them into following wrong teachings and doings. That is what the serpent did to Adam and Eve. All of God's creation is important to Him, and all was created with a specific purpose designed by God. Although, this book focuses on women, it is written to everyone. The goal of this book is to help everyone see that God has something for them to do, and chances are they will not be fulfilled or happy until they are doing what God created them to do. Women especially are being pushed back, criticized, ignored, silenced, and abused in today's churches. The majority of Christian women are being emotionally abused by their husbands over church people and church matters. Christian women and their children are suffering due to man's ignorance.

This book is written to encourage women that they are somebody; that they matter to God; and that they have callings given to them directly from God. This book's goal is to show women that just by being a woman there are certain things that only they can do and certain ministries that only they can fulfill. The ministry of motherhood is exclusive to a woman. Not only is motherhood exclusive, but what God tells a woman to do specifically is exclusive to her also. No one else should do what God created a particular person to do. The impact is not the same.

Mainly, this book is written to encourage everyone, especially women to seek God and find the purpose in which they were created. After finding their purpose, then they should get busy doing what God wants them to do. In other words, people should let God define them, not man.

INTRODUCTION

After receiving the revelation from the Holy Spirit that a woman is just as precious and important to God as a man and that a woman is created with divine purpose for God's use, I have been compelled to show some significant callings and to show some significant roles that God used women to play in the Scriptures throughout the Bible. God created everything for a divine purpose. Women have evolved over thousands of years. They have come from being quiet keepers at home who could be passed around from man to man and treated anyway the man wanted to treat them to striving independent successful business women, working women, and in many cases heads of their households with everything and everyone in the house depending on them to make it through their daily lives. Through observation I know that in the Black community and other communities, it is clear that women outnumber men in the church; therefore, we can assume that women make themselves more available to God to be used by Him. As a matter of fact, it is often said that the women keep the church in operation because of their willingness and their strong drive to serve the LORD. Many churches do not have enough men who attend church on a consistent basis to do anything.

I discovered that a vast number of women are unhappy due to restraints placed on them in ministry. I found that this problem exists not only in America but throughout the world. There are several articles and books that have been published about unhappy women in ministry. In my reading, I found that women are unhappy due to the fact that they have been dehumanized by people and mostly husbands who are pastors. Surveys by the Global Pastors Wives Network show that 80 percent of pastors' wives feel left out and unappreciated by church members. There are organizations that have been established just for pastors' wives, such as the League of Pastors' Wives and Other Women in the Ministry. These organizations were formed to minister to the frustrations that women feel dealing with ministry. Also, there are a great numbers of testimonies that have been given by pastors' wives expressing their feelings of loneliness, verbal abuse and sometimes physical abuse which can come due to verbal abuse. Yet, another survey show that 85 percent of pastors' wives are depressed. One writer wrote that a number of pastor's wives sometimes go from active members in the church to wallflowers. In other words, during the beginning of their ministry the pastor's wife wore many hats. After a few members came and expressed their desire to do what she was doing, the pastor, her husband told her to sit in the church, be seen, look happy, and say nothing no matter what happens. I too have this testimony; therefore, I know what it is like to be a woman who has given her all to a man and his vision in ministry only to receive much grief and unhappiness in the end. Therefore, I am compelled to write to all the people who use the Word of God and the church to misuse and mistreat women who are called by God for specific divine ministry.

First, this book is written to all the women who are confused and uncertain about their roles in ministry. Secondly, to all the women who started out in ministry and somewhere lost their way because of circumstances, such as divorce or something else that happened to take away their determination to fulfill their call by God in their lives. Thirdly, to the women that have never understood that God's reason for creating them is for them to do the work of ministry in some appropriate capacity. Last but not least, to all the men who seem to not have the understanding that God's Word is clear and true; that God has no respecter of persons; that women were not created for just men; and that everyone has a place in ministry especially women. By using the phrase especially women, I mean that God used only a woman to bring the most important human being there ever was, has been, or ever will be into the world. Man had absolutely no role to play in the ministry of Jesus' entrance into the world. It was God and only the woman, Mary. Also, without women, men could not replenish the earth alone, nor would they have the help that God created for them in the beginning.

Also most importantly, to both men and women who have not discerned that everyone has their specific place in ministry that should encompass their daily lives and build them into who they really are supposed to become. When they are not allowed to operate in their callings or they are made to feel suppressed and oppressed by men and women, the Holy Spirit is being quenched, and women are becoming men's slaves instead of God's servants. Women need to settle in their minds that they belong to God; that He is their Lord; and that they are set apart for the Master's use. Women do not need men or other women dictating to them their fate; only God should be allowed to do that. Everyone deserves to feel that they are doing the good, acceptable, and perfect will of God in their lives. They deserve to feel fulfilled and happy in Christ. Women cannot be happy when they are not allowed to operate in their ministry calling properly or when they are looked at as if they are wrong by walking in their calling.

Women play several different important roles in society and in life generally. They are keepers at home, mothers, teachers, and leaders. All of these roles require that a woman be a servant to her family first of all and then to others, because she has had training at home that allows her to servant others. In other words, what she gives herself to the most is what she becomes. As homemakers, women are to provide 'the woman touch' that a home desperately needs. 'The woman touch' simply means putting tender loving care (TLC) in the home. She serves as the cleaning woman, the cook, and the caregiver. She is a teacher, a listener, a counselor, a disciplinarian, and a nurse to her children. She serves her spouse as well in areas such as listening, advising, and helping to provide for the family. Some serves as household secretaries, administrators, and in whatever capacities the business affairs of the household need whether she works outside the home or only at home. Women do what is necessary to manage their households. Most women seem to be more understanding and giving. They make tremendous sacrifices for their families and give their time and talents unconditionally without even considering their own needs and desires for their families. It is not outlandish to assume that a mother or wife will easily give up her life for her family.

With all that has been said of women, it is important to understand what God's purpose is for each individual woman. Every Christian woman needs to know what God wants her to do and who He wants her to be and become. In this book, we are going to look at what I think is God's whole purpose for women and also for men too. I am sure that you have heard that the woman was created for man. That thought is somewhat true. God did create woman or He pulled the female out of the male, because He did not want man to be alone according to Genesis 2:18. But God created all things including man and woman for Himself. The single most important purpose for all people is to be carriers of God's Word through obedience to God. We are commanded to obey and keep the laws and commandments of God; this message is clear from the beginning and all the way through to the end of the Bible.

Since it is our belief that the Holy Scripture was written to us as a guide for us to live by and follow, we should examine and study them to gain an understanding as to how women should conduct themselves when it comes to carrying out God's Plan for them. By reading this book I pray that you will clearly see that women carried the Word of God from the beginning to the end of the Bible. Women unquestionable callings are mothers and wives. No man can play these roles just as no woman can be fathers and husbands. This book will highlight some of the women God used to fulfill His plan in the earth. It will look at the women in their roles as mothers, wives, leaders, and ministers carrying out God's Word. It will show that God purposely looked for certain women at varies times with a specific assignment that only those women could fulfill. Most of the women this book describes will portray God using them in the ministry of motherhood. Some will be portrayed as women used by God in the ministry of war and governmental decisions. Others will be highlighted as women used by God in the ministry gifts of the fivefold ministry found in the New International Version Bible in Ephesians 4:11 **"It was he who gave some to be apostles, some to be prophets, some to be evangelists, and some to be pastors and teachers (NIV)."** Of course, most if not all of these will fit somewhere in the last description as ministers of God.

A Calling of
Motherhood

Chapter 1

Eve, The Mother of all living things

Note that in the first Chapter of Genesis, God made man in His own image and called man male and female (Verse 27, NIV). We get the idea here that man was asexual which means that he could reproduce his image alone; there was only one sex not two. God told man to replenish the earth, but later in Genesis, Chapter 2 after He brought all the animals to man to name, there were none there like man. **"The LORD God said, 'It is not good for the man to be alone I will make a helper suitable for him' (Verse 18, NIV)."** Then God caused man to sleep while He pulled woman out of him. In other words, He took one person, the man and made him into two people, man and woman or male and female.

The first woman that God created was Eve. This story is found in the Book of Genesis, Chapter 2: 20-22. After God brought all the animals to Adam to name, the Bible states, **". . . . But for Adam no suitable helper was found. So the Lord God caused the man to fall into a deep sleep; and while he was sleeping, He took one of the man's ribs and closed up the place with flesh. Then the Lord God made the woman from the rib He had taken out of the man, and He brought her to the man (NIV)."** Here the Bible is clear in the fact that God took the time to make a woman. He didn't just form her out of the dust of the ground like He did the man, because He had already placed the woman inside the man. He pulled her out of man by taking the man's rib. I am sure that you have heard the sermons that have been preached and taught that woman is supposed to be by the man's side because the rib came from his side. Not just any woman, his wife is a helper suitable for him. Adam's wife was created to help him and to be a companion to him. Adam himself said, **"This (Eve) is now bone of my bone and flesh of my flesh; she shall be called woman, for she was taken out of man. For this reason a man will leave his father and mother and be united to his wife, and they will become one flesh (Verses 23&24, NIV)."** Thus, we see the first covenant between humans formed. Just as God the father, Jesus the son, and the Holy Spirit are one, man and woman were one. Also, this is why Paul could easily say, **"Husbands, love your wives, just as Christ loved the church and gave himself up for her (Ephesians 5:25, NIV)."** While man was in his perfect state of being without flaws, he was one with his wife. God made both of them as one flesh, one spiritual being separated into two people to be companions to one another. Men ought to love their wives as if they love their own bodies, because she is a part of his body or his make-up. She is who makes him complete in a sense. The wife is the part of the man that fulfills everything that he cannot do by himself that God commanded him to do. For example, he cannot replenish the earth by himself. **"In this same way, husbands ought to love their wives as their own bodies. He who loves his wife loves himself (Ephesians 5:28, NIV)."** From these verses we get a very clear picture of the men who do not love their wives. They do not love themselves; therefore, it is my belief that they take their frustrations with themselves out on their wives.

Later, we see the serpent approaching Eve and talking to her to convince her to disobey God's command. In Chapter 3: 1-7, the serpent raised a question in the woman's mind, **"Did God really say, 'You must not eat from any tree in the garden'?"** The woman's reply was that **"God did say that you must not eat from the tree in the middle of the garden."** Then she added a little to what God had said by saying, **"You must not touch it, or you will die (Verse 3, NIV)."** The serpent said **"you will not surely die . . . For God knows that when you eat of it your eyes will be opened, and you will be like**

God, knowing good and evil (Verses 4 & 5, NIV)." Satan knew what God had said and he probably used the add-on the woman said to be more convincing in his quest to corrupt God's man and woman. That is why we should make sure that we know and quote the Word correctly, because Satan will use our very words and thoughts to create confusion in our minds to manipulate us into believing what he wants us to believe. After he confuses our thoughts, then he knows that he has us. But, this should be the time that we really search the Scriptures to clear up our confusion by learning what did God really say. We can find the answer to this question in the Word of God or simply by going to God in prayer and asking Him to clear up the confusion. At that point, Adam and Eve should have consulted with God.

The serpent caused the woman to pause and think about what he was saying. Also, he caused her to doubt and question God's command in her mind. After all she did not know what was meant by dying anyway. Because Satan's plan to be just like the all-knowing God and even above God did not work out for him; he caused the woman to desire to know the wisdom that God knows. After she thought about it and mediated on what the serpent said, she looked at the tree, and it looked better to her than it ever did before. She saw that the tree was good for food and she strongly desired it. Eve was looking at the fruit differently now; she ate it not only because it was food, but also to become wise. The serpent's power to persuade won her over to Satan's side. Then she gave some to her husband who was there with her, and he ate too.

Both of their eyes were opened, and they knew that they were naked. Immediately man and woman began to have negative feelings and emotions. They began to feel ashamed and fearful. They felt that they had to hide their nakedness. Man and woman felt the need to hide from God and the need to cover up their disobedience (sin) which was symbolic of covering their bodies with fig leaves. Before they sinned, they did not even know that they were naked, and they had no negative feelings and emotions. They were perfect, and they had a wonderful peaceful secure relationship with God. We know this because they became aware that their bodies were uncovered after they sinned. God had them covered in his glory. Being covered in God's glory is a wonderful, peaceful place and state of mind. When we get into His presence there are no worries or cares, because we know that the devil can't touch us in God's presence. As a matter of fact, thoughts about the devil do not enter into our minds at all when we are in God's presence.

Yes, immediately afterward man and woman knew something happened. They knew that they were not covered anymore and that they felt the evilness of what they had done, that is when fear entered into their feelings and emotions. Uneasiness began to flood their minds because they could feel a break in their relationship with God. It's just like when we disobey our parents, we feel bad about it and try to hide our disobedience. We feel ashamed and guilty about what we did and hope that our parents never find out about it. But, in the back of our minds we know that the truth will come to light one day. Satan taunts us by reminding us of what we did until the truth is told. The fear of our parents finding out is very present; it was the same way for Adam and Eve. They heard God's voice walking in the garden, and they hid from Him. God asked, **"Adam where are you?"** Notice, God called them both Adam because he saw them as one.

When they presented themselves to God, Adam said to God that he was afraid because he was naked, so he hid himself. Then God asked him, **"Who told you that you were naked? Have you eaten from the tree that I commanded you not to eat from (Genesis 3:11, NIV)?"** The man answered, **"The woman you put here with me— she gave me some fruit from the tree and I ate it".** Then the Lord God said to the woman, **"What is this you have done? The woman said, "The serpent deceived me, and I ate it (Verses 12-14, NIV)."** The woman realized that she had been tricked into doing wrong. They should have known that God is all knowing and that they could not hide anything from Him. It was His routine to come and fellowship with them. Just like God questioned them and got their true story, our parents sometimes seem to know just how to question us and get to the truth. They confessed their sin.

Just as we have to discipline our children when they do wrong, God had to discipline Adam, Eve, and the serpent. All three took part in the sin and all three of them had to be punished. God had already told them that the day that they ate of the tree, they would die. Since God is a spirit and he does not and cannot lie, death began the moment that they ate of the tree. No, they did not drop dead that moment, an hour later, or even years later, but they did experience a cut off of the glory that was surrounding them. We know this because they looked down at themselves and saw their naked bodies instead of the glory cloud that was covering their bodies. Not only that, they tried to hide from the presence of God, because some deterioration of the relationship with God had taken place. God's presence or glory cannot stay or dwell in the midst of sin. A spiritual covering over their bodies had been removed. Since God is the life supplier, they had cut off some of the lines that connected them directly into God; therefore, they started their journey of death spiritually. Their journey would take hundreds of years before their physical bodies would return to dust, but nevertheless they would surely die just as God told them they would.

Then God spoke the punishment each one would receive. He told the serpent what would be his fate on earth from now to eternity. God said that because you have done this, cursed are you above all the animals. The part of the serpent's punishment that I want to highlight is that God told him that He would put enmity (ill-will; hostility) between him and the woman, and between his offspring and hers; her offspring will crush his head, and his offspring will strike her offspring's heel.

God told the serpent that since he deceived the woman and convinced her to disobey His command; He would make the woman and her seed his worst enemy. Her seed will crush the serpent's seed head. In other words, serpents will always be on the ground slithering and sneaking around trying to bite man's heel and infiltrating poison in his mind and body. The poison that the serpent possesses will kill man spiritually and eventually physically by the things that he allows to enter into his mind through the serpent's words. For example, when one allows himself to be flattered to the point of hurting others to lift himself and the ones that flattered him up, he has been poisoned by the devil's lies, and he is walking in spiritual death. Even in the natural a non-poisonous serpent's secretions will cause someone to swell and to be sick when it bites. In other words, those serpents that you think are harmless are still serpents that are cursed above all animals and their words cannot bring anything but destruction.

In today's world, the spirit of the serpent lives in men and women, because Satan uses whoever he can to cause man to die, to be destroyed, and to be stolen from (John 10:10). The devil through the serpent stole eternal life from mankind and caused mankind to live a life that leads to destruction and death unless he is in Christ. This is mankind's fate throughout all generations until the final judgment. Today, Satan is not using animals to deceive men and women, he is using men and women to deceive and destroy each other. There is nothing new under the sun. Presently, through man Satan is still saying to man and woman, **'Did God really say that?'** There are men and women who seem to have a gift of manipulating others. They are very convincing, and believe it or not, they display themselves as God's saints. Some people are clever at convincing other people and making them believe that God does not require what He really requires of them.

On the day that God spoke to the serpent and told him that the woman's seed will bruise his head, He placed a very serious calling and responsibility on the woman in child bearing and child rearing. Notice when God spoke the punishment to the woman, it was mainly about her pains and suffering due to having children. All mothers know that the pain does not end with the actual birth, because mothers bear their children's pain in their hearts for the rest of their lives. From the time of their child's birth until the end of their life or their child's life, mothers go far and beyond the call of duty to see that their child's needs are met no matter how old the child becomes. God told the woman that He would greatly increase her pains in childbearing; and with pain she will give birth to children.

Little did the woman know when she so desired to be like God by knowing good and evil and by acting to fulfill her desire; she was accepting the experience of evil into herself and all womankind throughout all generations. The woman desired to be like God, but in reality she became like Satan knowing evil, up until that point she knew nothing but good. She was already like God made in his image and likeness. It is evil to experience pain in any form. Mothers experience physical pains, psychological pains, and emotional pains while going through the duration period of pregnancy and afterward, because there are all kinds of changes that take place in their bodies and all kinds of thoughts going through their minds. For example, chemical imbalances are happening; parts of her body are stretching and emotions are heightening. This is why mothers can be extremely excited during pregnancy and right after birth they yet feel ashamed, frustrated, and embarrassed. They go from emotional highs to emotional lows (depression) in matter of minutes. There is also a spiritual transformation taking place in her, because having a baby is really supernatural. It may seem natural, because it happens often with humans and animals, but only God can perform the process.

There are so many emotions and feelings that come to taunt her. In most cases after she finds out that she is pregnant, she begins to take care of herself as a means of taking care of and protecting the seed that she is carrying. She often prays whether she was a praying woman before pregnancy or not, because she understands that carrying a child is a spiritual, godly intervention that only God can cause. Most mothers draw near to God during pregnancy through conversation with or prayer to him. They know that He is the life giver and the life supplier. Mothers become very concern about their babies' well-being. Many questions enter their minds. They find themselves wondering and hoping that everything about their babies will be normal and well. They have about nine to ten months or about 38 to 40 weeks to ponder these things in their minds and hearts until they can actually physically see and hold the miracle that God allows them to bring forth into the earth with His help. Excuse me for a moment while I give Him praise. AIN'T GOD AWESOME? HALLELUJAH! GLORY TO HIS NAME! A vast majority of mothers thank God for bringing them through pregnancy and childbirth, because the whole process could have been detrimental to both the mother and/or the baby. There are many cases where mothers have died during childbirth and even more cases where the baby did not survive. Becoming a mother is phenomenal.

The second part of the woman punishment was that her desire will be for her husband, and he will rule over her. This part of the curse has proven to be devastating for women too, because men have taken this fact and used it to abuse their wives in every way that they can be abused. Husbands make their wives subjects to them. Some set themselves up as kings and expect their wives to serve them in every capacity, and when their wives refuse the commands or refuse to allow themselves to be mistreated, husbands talk about them and seek a divorce. Women are abused emotionally, physically, and sometimes sexually by their husbands. In many cases, wives become ex-wives and are left with the responsibility of children and debt that their husbands made. Unfortunately, not only do worldly men use this Scripture for their benefit, but Christians are worse than they are, speaking from experience. I cannot begin to tell you how many times that I heard that the husband or man is the head of the household, and he has the biblical rights to make the final decisions. As I reflect back, I see clearly that there were hardly any compromise and many bad outcomes due to him making the final decisions. Women including me knew that the decisions were bad but gave in to them, because the Scripture was used, **"The head of the woman is man (I Corinthians 11: 3, NIV)."** In reality men really use this Scripture to get their way.

After the punishments were given, Adam named his wife Eve, and said that she is the mother of all the living. This indicates origination or first which says that Eve was the first on earth to become a mother. Then God put them out of the Garden of Even. Chapter 4 says that Adam knew his wife or had sex with her, and she gave birth to a son that they named Cain. She had a second son name Abel. After her two sons grew up, they brought offerings to God. God was pleased with Abel's offering and received it, but He was displeased with Cain's offering and rejected it. Because of this Eve experienced a physical death when Cain, her oldest son killed Abel, her youngest son because of jealousy and envy. Cain hated Abel because God was pleased with his offering. Then God had to punish Cain, which caused him to become a wanderer. I cannot begin to imagine how much hurt Eve felt after this incident. She basically had lost both of her sons, because although Cain was physically alive, I am convinced that his relationship with his parents was strained emotionally. Because he was a wanderer, this is evident that he ceased to live near his parents which indicate that he cut himself off from them.

We know that Eve was the first to experience motherhood, and now we can conclude that she was the first to experience pain, a broken heart and the burden of her children's fate for the rest of her life. Wow, what a harsh punishment this mother had to endure, because she ate of the tree that God told her not to eat of which caused sin and death to be allowed in the earth. Adam and Eve were not the first to physically die, but their son was. The last time the Bible mentions Eve is in Genesis, Chapter 4, verse 25, **"Adam lay with his wife again, and she gave birth to a son and named him Seth, saying, 'God has granted me another child in place of Abel, since Cain killed him (NIV).'"** This verse shows that Eve's heart was very much grieved over Abel and Cain. Her statement after the birth of Seth clearly depicts her mind being consumed with thoughts of the tragedy that took place between her sons. Seth probably was given to her as a mean for some of her emotional healing. God provided her with another son that she could love and nurture; that she could embrace and wrap her heart around; that she could train up not to go the way that his brother, Cain did; and that needed her to have her mind not to be consumed with Cain and Abel, but needed her mind to be occupied on him, concentrating on taking care of his needs. Because like any mother, Eve probably spent her days and nights wondering what possessed Cain to do what he did? She probably blamed herself in the way that she reared him or just maybe she did not say the right things to him. She may have even thought that she did not give him or even show him enough love; but at the same time, she wondered why Abel had to die. Eve probably thought and asked God why it was not her that was killed instead of her son, Abel? We could speculate that she had many thoughts while longing to have her sons back at home with her living in peace and harmony, but we know that was not possible after the occurrence of the tragedy. Like most mothers, every one of Eve's children was important to her. All of them held their own special place in her heart, and she loved them equally. Although Cain murdered his brother, Eve still loved him.

The first woman's story seems very sad, but we need to keep in mind that God restored some happiness and joy that was brought to her in the form of another baby boy. A mother's children are her pride and joy. She boasts about her children often, and she takes pride in their good qualities even if their character is not good. As sad as it may seem, God spoke purpose and destiny to Eve when He told her that He would use her and her seed to defeat the devil. The devil heard what God said to the woman; therefore, he releases all of his evil forces against the women. Women endure so many pains and hardships; not only in childbearing, but also in marriage or couple relationships with their spouses or partners. Just as God gave Eve hope and an expected future to look forward to with her new baby boy and a promise of what her seed would do, God gives women today that same hope. Every woman can experience God's plan for her life by drawing close to Him and seeking His purpose. When God gives us directions and commands, we must follow them and obey them without questioning Him. Our first love must be God, and we must love Him more than anyone else which is the first commandment. We must have a willing and submissive heart toward God and His plan for our lives.

Chapter 2

Sarah

The next woman that God spoke to and used was introduced in Genesis 12 beginning at verse 10. There was a famine in the land, so Abram and his wife Sarai went to live in Egypt for a while. Abram said to his wife, **"I know what a beautiful woman you are. When the Egyptians see you, they will say, 'This is his wife.' Then they will kill me but will let you live. Say you are my sister, so that I will be treated well for your sake and my life will be spared because of you (Genesis12:11-13, NIV)."** Sure enough when they arrived into Egypt, Sarai's beauty demanded the attention of Pharaoh's officials, and they told Pharaoh how beautiful she was. She was taken into the palace, and Abram was treated well for her sake. As a matter of fact, Abram was treated so well because of Sarai that he was given enough cattle, sheep, donkeys, camels, and men and women servants to make him wealthy. WOW! The LORD protected Sarai and kept Pharaoh from violating her by inflicting serious diseases on Pharaoh and his household. After Pharaoh realized that Sarai was Abram's wife, he summoned Abram and rebuked him for not telling him the truth. He sent orders to his men to send Abram, Sarai, and everything they had been given away from him and his kingdom. **"So Abram went up from Egypt to the Negev, with his wife and everything he had, and Lot went with him. Abram had become very wealthy in livestock and in silver and gold (Gen. 13:1-2, NIV)."**

This story describes Sarai as a very beautiful woman in appearance. Just a glance at her made men pay attention. The Bible says that Pharaoh's officials who first saw her coming into Egypt with Abram went to Pharaoh and praised her to Pharaoh because of her beauty. It was customary in that time for the Pharoah to have the best of the best; therefore, he took the most beautiful women for himself to be his wives. Sarai did not only have outward beauty, she possessed inward beauty as well. We can see from her acts of humility and obedience to her husband that she was beautiful inside too. Evidently, she said very little to the Egyptians other than what Abram told her to say. She humbly submitted herself to the will of her husband and allowed herself to be submitted and committed to another man's desires in order to save her husband's life. Sarai had to have trusted what Abram told her, because Pharaoh could have killed her for lying to him too; she really risked her own life for Abram. What a brave and courageous thing Sarai did!

Notice that the story also says that Abram was treated well because of Sarai; because of Sarai, Abram became wealthy. While Pharaoh was thinking that Abram was her brother, he treated him very well. Pharaoh sought to please Sarai by treating who he thought to be her brother well; therefore, he showered him with gifts. I am sure that Sarai was given all the things that a queen would have too which may explain the silver and gold that Abram obtained. How often do we see in today's society men gaining from their wives materials things and wealth only to end up mistreating and abusing their wives? I have experienced this and witnessed many wives and significant others pouring themselves out and making so many sacrifices to help their husbands and significant others to: get on their feet, gain a career, get a meaningful job or just gain better financial status in life only to end up being mistreated and unappreciated. People often say that a lot of women are only attracted to men that have means to support them and that should be so. In today's world some men are seeking out women who can take care of them, but this was not the case for Sarai. As we follow her life we will see that she did not live happily ever after this big event, but she was treated well by her husband.

The most important detail in this story is that God was with Sarai, and he protected her through the whole ordeal. **"But the LORD inflicted serious diseases on Pharaoh and his household because of Abram's wife Sarai. So Pharaoh summoned Abram. 'What have you done to me?' he said. 'Why didn't you tell me she was your wife? Why did you say, 'She is my sister,' so that I took her to be my wife? Now then, here is your wife. Take her and go (Gen. 12: 17-19, NIV)!"** God would not let any harm come to Sarai from Pharaoh, nor would he allow Pharaoh to violate her in any kind of way. He allowed Sarai to be used to gain wealth for Abram and herself, and at the same time, he kept a protective shield around her that no man, not even the Pharaoh, could break through. Because God had a specific plan and purpose for Sarai, he kept her under his wings; he sheltered her and shielded her throughout her life.

Sarai and Hagar

In the sixteenth chapter of Genesis, Sarai decides that since she had not been able to have a child she would give her maid servant to Abram to have a son. During that time it was customary for the wife of a man who could not have children to have children through their maid servant. Hagar's child would be considered and raised as Sarai's child. Abram agreed. So, she gives Hagar to him as his wife. After Hagar become pregnant, she begins to despise Sarai. Sarai sees that Hagar is a person that has negative feelings which she begins to display toward her. Hagar shows her that she is not a puppet that she can just pull her string when she wants some kind of performance out of her and when she does not want her to perform, she can just put her on the shelf. Sarai tells Abram that it is his fault that her servant Hagar cannot stand her. She says that she put Hagar in his arms to be used for her sake not just his sake. In other words, Hagar thought that she had risen above or perhaps thought she was equal to her mistress since she was able to give Abram something that Sarai couldn't, and after all, she was his wife too. I am sure that she thought that she did not have to do what Sarai asked her to do anymore. But, Sarai became very distraught with her attitude and took a very strong stand against it with Abram. She saw that if she allowed Hagar to continue in her disrespect toward her, the relationship between she and her husband would be in trouble for the rest of their lives together. To prove to Sarai that his loyalty and love was only to her, Abram tells Sarai to do with Hagar, her servant, whatever she wants to.

Sarai begins to mistreat Hagar because Hagar is not submissive to her. One translation said that Sarai beat her. Hagar runs away; but, God knows and sees all things. God sent an angel to look for her. The angel found her in the desert by a spring and addressed her by her name and her ministry (place in life). He said to her in Genesis 16:7, **"Hagar, servant of Sarai, where have you come from, and where are you going (NIV)?"** She tells the angel that she is running away from Sarai. When the angel spoke to her, he identified her as Sarai's servant. The angel told her that a servant is who she is; therefore, she is to go back and submit herself to Sarai. The angel tells her also that she is pregnant and that the LORD will increase her descendants to a number too big to count. He further adds that she would have a son and his name will be Ishmael, because the LORD heard and saw her misery. I believe that the angel told her about her misery with a promise that she will not have to be miserable always; her deliverance would come. Her son will be wild, his hand will be against everyone, everyone's hand will be against him, and he will always have hostility toward all of his brothers. Wow! What a prophecy to speak over someone's child. Perhaps, Ishmael's fate or calling was such as this because he was man's idea (Sarai and Abram) not God's idea. Everything that is done outside of God causes misery and pain. Everything that is done outside of God's will is wrong and suffers harsh consequences. We know that still today Ishmael's descendants are against Isaac's descendants, and they are fighting wars among themselves.

Evidently, Hagar obeyed the angel by going back and submitting herself to Sarai, but after Sarah gave birth to Isaac who was truly the child that God promised Abram, there were major conflicts between Sarai and Hagar again. They probably had conflict since the time that Hagar became pregnant, but they were tolerating each other for the sake of Abraham's son, Ishmael, who Sarai was supposing to be raising as her own. It is almost unbelievable, how she showed him no mercy when she saw that he was mocking or opposing her son, Isaac.

The tension between Sarai and Hagar had built up over the process of years, and by this time, they probably hated each other. A celebration took place because of Isaac. Ishmael who was about 14 years old at this time mocked Isaac. He made fun of him and Sarai saw him; she demanded that Abram get rid of Hagar and her son. Abraham was very troubled by the fact that Sarah wanted him to send his son away, but God told him to do as his wife had asked him to do. God also told him that He would take care of the child and that nations would come from him. Abraham knew God was true to his Word after all He gave him the same promise, and it was in the process of coming to pass.

At that point in their lives, I believe that Sarah knew in order for her son and her to have peaceful lives, Hagar and Ishmael could not be a part of their family any longer. There were much tension between Hagar and her; beside that, Ismael would probably have been an antagonist to Isaac as he grew up. Everyone knew that Isaac was the promised child; Ishmael had already begun to show that he was somewhat jealous and envious of him. We know that jealousy and envy only lead to hatred; therefore, we cannot begin to imagine what a troubled life Isaac would have had growing up with an older brother who hated him. His life may have ended like Abel in an early death. Sarah being a mother whose instinct now was to protect her child had to get rid of the people that would be there to destroy him, because she saw the envy that Ishmael displayed toward him while he was just a little baby. Isaac's name means laughter; by him having to grow up with Ismael would have probably taken the laughter away from him, and his destination was tied up in the meaning of his name. When one has to take ridicule and being poked at, it kills one's self-esteem and self-worth. It was at that point that Sarah saw that she had made a tremendous mistake by inserting her opinion, thoughts, and plan into God's equation of making a great nation out of Abram through his seed. She saw that the only way to correct her mistake was to demand that Hagar and Ishmael be sent away. Although Ishmael was vanished from growing up with Isaac, he will live on through his seed to be opposing to Isaac's seed until God comes back to get us.

Like Sarai, women of God, we sometimes execute ideas and plans that are not God's ideas and plans for us. After recognizing that the plans are not what God intended for us, we need to immediate get rid of the things or people that will destroy our lives. Pastor's wives especially sit and watch their husbands put men and women into different positions in the church, and they surround themselves with these people that are very serious threats to their marriage, family, and ultimately to their ministry. Their husbands often become so entangled with such people, until they unfortunately most of the time lose their family, credibility, and ministry. Their wives and children become scarred for the rest of their lives, because most men do not consult God when their wives tell them to send certain people away from them, or their wives can see the destruction but are afraid of hurting other's feelings never say anything to them. When God shows you that the thief has come to live in your house, it is your responsibility to try to get him out, or you will be put out of your own home and your children will suffer.

Abraham gave Hagar food and water and sent her away. After Hagar had wandered in the desert until her food and water ran out, she gave the last of the water to her son and placed him under a bush. Then she walked away from him according to the Bible about the distant of a bow and arrow shot. She sat down and began to cry out to the LORD. Her prayer was that she would not see her son die. The LORD spoke to her. He asked her what was the matter with her and told her that he heard the child crying. God promised her before Ishmael was born that a nation would come from him. She saw and talked with the LORD at that time and should have known that God was with her and her son. The Lord opened her eyes and she saw water. Afterward the Bible says that the boy grew and became an awesome archer, which meant that he was a provider for his mother and himself. After that Hagar went to Egypt and chose him a wife, and the great nation did come from him which is in existence today. It is also important to note that through this situation, Hagar became a free woman and a queen in her own right. Because God saw her misery and pain, He freed her and caused her and her son to prosper.

As we follow the life of Sarai, God eventually changes her name to Sarah which means that He had established a covenant with her. He gave her part of his name by changing the *i* at the end to a*h therefore forming the name Sarah* (ah is one of God's names). We see that the

Pharaoh was not the only one who took Sarah to be his wife; this happened a second time to her later in her life when they moved to Gerar. **"Then Abimelech king of Gerar sent for Sarah and took her. But God came to Abimelech in a dream one night and said to him, 'You are as good as dead because of the woman you have taken; she is a married woman (Gen. 20: 2-3, NIV).'"** Here we see that God was very serious about protecting Sarah, and He made it very clear to the king in his dream. Of course, Abimelech told God that he acted out of innocent and that he did not know that they were married because they both told him that they were siblings. The LORD in turn told him that He knew what he was saying was true and that He was keeping him from sinning by not letting him touch Sarah. Then God told Abimelech to return the man's wife, for he (Abraham) is a prophet, and he will pray for him and he (Abimelech) will live. **"But if you do not return her, you may be sure that you and all yours will die (Gen. 20: 7, NIV)."** The morning after Abimelech's dream, he told all of his officials and they were afraid. Then he summoned Abraham and asked him why he wronged him by telling him that Sarah was his sister. Abraham told him that he told Sarah to tell this to others when they move from one place to another place, and this is how she will show her love for him. Abraham also said that he felt that Gerar was not a God fearing place; therefore, he feared for his life. So, they told the half-truth in order for him to keep his life. He and Sarah shared the same father but not the same mother; therefore, they were siblings.

"And Abimelech took sheep, and oxen and menservants, and womenservants, and gave them unto Abraham, and restored him Sarah his wife. And Abimelech said, Behold, my land is before thee: dwell where it pleaseth thee. And unto Sarah he said, I have given thy brother a thousand pieces of silver: behold, he is to thee a covering of the eyes, unto all that are with thee, and with all other: thus she was reproved. So Abraham prayed unto God: and God healed Abimelech, and his wife, and his maidservants; and they bare children. For the LORD had fast closed up all the wombs of the house of Abimelech, because of Sarah Abraham's wife (Genesis 20:14-18, KJV)." God was protecting Sarah the whole time that she was in Abimelech's house. He was with her just like He is with many women today in their situations and predicaments that are not ordained by God. God had a specific purpose for Sarah, and He saw to it that other men did not defile her. He kept her safe in the midst of her storms. I am a witness that God will first of all keep you safe in the midst of a trouble storm and He will surely bring you out of it. No storm is too great that God cannot deliver you from.

In Genesis, Chapter 21, God fulfilled the promise that He made to Sarah. Sarah was a strong courteous woman who through a determination and a strong desire to please God and her husband did what was necessary to protect and raise the seed that God allowed her to bare. During her life, she learned that who God chose was the one He used to fulfill what He wanted. God promised Abraham a son that would come from Sarah, because she was his wife. Everyone outside of the marriage was foreign and did not belong and could not mesh within; therefore, everyone that was born outside of the original union could be nothing but wild, bitter, and angry. This was what Sarah had to deal with in the situations with Hagar and Ishmael. I am sure that this situation was the most difficult one in her lifetime that she had to overcome, but she did. So Sarah, God's chosen woman accomplished the mission that God set before her, but not without trials, pains, and tribulations. After reaching one hundred twenty-seven years old in age, Sarah died. Sarah the mother of many nations had fulfilled her calling by leaving the promised child to carry on her legacy to generations from then to eternity.

Chapter 3

Rebekah

After Sarah died, Abraham made his servant swear that he would go back to his country and find Isaac a wife from among his relatives, because he could not have a wife from the Canaanites. His servant was a little reluctant at first because he was not sure that a stranger would follow him back without Isaac being with him. But, Abraham told him that the LORD would send an angel before him to choose the one; therefore, God looked for a woman who would be Isaac's wife. Upon the arrival in Abraham's father country, the servant prayed and asked God to let him know who was the chosen woman by causing her to give him and his camels water until they were filled. As soon as he finished praying, Rebekah came to the well where the servant was at. He saw that she was very beautiful, and he asked her for a drink of water. After giving him water, she told him that she would water his camels too. She drew water from the well and poured it into a trough for the camels until they were filled. The servant observed her as she fulfilled the request that he had asked the LORD. Then the servant gave her a gold earring and two golden bracelets that were worth a lot of money.

Then he asked her who her father was and required as to whether or not he would let him stay the night at his house. Rebekah told him that she was the daughter of Milcah and Bethuel, the son of Nahor, Abraham's brother. She told him that there was enough room for him to stay and that there was straw and food enough to feed his camels.

Then she ran ahead of him to her mother's house to tell about the man that she had just met at the well.

Rebekah had a brother name Laban, and when he saw the gold earring and the bracelets, he went out to the man at the well, greeted him as one who is blessed of the LORD and told him that he had prepared a room for him. Laban also told him that there was room and food prepared and waiting for his camels too. After the servant went into their house, they gave him and the men with him water to wash their feet. Then they set meat before them to eat. But, the servant would not eat until he told them why he had come. He told them that he was Abraham's servant and that his master was greatly blessed by the LORD. He said that Abraham had become great, because the LORD had given him sheep, cattle, silver, gold, camels, donkeys, menservants and maidservants. He told them that Abraham's wife Sarah had borne Abraham a son in their old age, and his master Abraham had sent him to his father's family after he made him swear to get a wife for his son, Isaac, because he could not marry anyone from the country in which they were living in. The servant told them that he was reluctant to come without Isaac, but Abraham told him that an angel of the LORD would go before him to cause the woman to come back with him. He also told them that he prayed and asked God to make his journey and day prosperous by letting the woman that he had chosen come out to the well and give him and his camels drink until they were filled. Before he could finish praying in his heart, Rebekah came out and did just what he asked the LORD to let her do. Then the servant said that he asked whose daughter was she, and she told him that she was the granddaughter of his master's brother, Nahor. He put the gold ring in her nose and the bracelets on her arm, and then he bowed down and worshiped the LORD, because the God of Abraham had put him on the right road and led him to the exact place and person whom he was seeking after. The servant asked if they would show kindness and faithfulness to Abraham by letting Rebekah become Isaac's wife. Bethuel and Laban replied that they knew that it was from the LORD; therefore, they consented.

The servant brought out many gifts for Rebekah, her brother, and her parents and gave them. Then her mother and brother asked if she could stay with them for ten more days, but the servant asked them not to detain him any longer. He needed to return to his master as soon as possible. They asked Rebekah was she willing to go with the man and the men with him and she consented. So, they blessed her and sent her along with her maids with the men.

When they arrived back to the country where Abraham was living, Isaac saw them approaching on camels while he was mediating in a field one evening. Rebekah saw him while approaching and asked who he was. The servant told her that he was his master. Then she covered her face with her veil, because he was coming to meet them. After the servant told Isaac about his journey and how the LORD led him straight to Rebekah, Isaac took her into his mother's tent and made her his wife. He loved her, and she comforted him after his mother's death.

We can clearly see that Rebekah was hand-picked and chosen by God to be Isaac's wife. When God choses someone, he looks for certain qualities and certain features about a person. We see the features when the Bible describes her as beautiful and a virgin. We see the qualities when we see her serving the servant of Abraham, the men that were with him, and the camels. Also, we can see how humble and caring she was when she filled pitcher of water after pitcher of water until even the camels were filled. The servant of Abraham stood and observed her servitude as she worked to water the animals. It must have been an awesome experience for him to ask God to do something specifically, and God did it just as he asked Him to do it. GLORY!

Because God was so involved in the choosing of Isaac's wife, this story shows that God is concern about the things that concern us. He is not a respecter of persons; especially when it comes to His own children. We are His children just as Abraham and Isaac were. God wants to help us in our everyday decisions. He wants to help us make all the right decisions and to help us surround ourselves with the right people. Christians should never choose a mate or even friends without God's consent. When we do things out of our own wills and make decisions without consulting God, we usually make a mess of things. Then, we find ourselves asking God what happened and why. But, we often come up with the same answer, because we didn't ask

God in the beginning. We live most of our young vibrant lives in a miserable marriage or some kind of relationship trying to hold on to something and someone that we should have let go of a long time ago; so we could get about our father's business. This doesn't only apply to marriages; sometimes, we hold on to people and/ or friends who have never meant us any good. When they enter into our lives, our world begins to slowly crumble around us. Yet we hold on to them not knowing that we should let go of them; until our world has completely fallen apart.

When we allow the wrong people to enter into our lives, they will cause our families to be torn and wounded. Our children will suffer in most cases. When men, especially men of God will not have the discernment to consult God about what to do or who to get rid of in their lives, usually, they end up with miserable lives and never can be satisfied.

This story also paints a beautiful picture of an earthly father caring so much for his son that he took the time to ask the LORD to choose a mate for him. Again, it is so important that you have the right mate and the right people around you. This is why Abraham did not want his son marrying any of the people around them. He wanted his son to have someone that had the same qualities and characteristics that his mother had. Abraham knew the stock in which his family was from. In other words, he knew what they believed; he knew the kindness of their hearts and he knew the humbleness that they could display. He also knew that they would obey and worship God; therefore, he wanted the best for his son. The best can only come from God.

We live in a world where children feel that their parents should have nothing to do with the choosing of their friends and surely should not even think that they should have an opinion about who they should marry. But, what children do not realize is that parents have gained a little knowledge and wisdom that they could not possibly have due to aging. Parents have lived on the earth a lot longer than they have and have had far more experiences than they have. Through wisdom they usually can tell whether or not someone will be a good companion to their children or even a friend. As a parent, there are certain types of people that I do not want my children to hang around with, and there are certain types of girls that I sure do not want for a daughter-in-law, because I know that certain types of people would only cause my sons to have miserable lives.

After Isaac and Rebekah became husband and wife, the next time the Bible mentioned Rebekah was when she began motherhood. In Genesis, Chapter 25: 21, the Bible says that Rebekah was barren, and Isaac prayed for her to the LORD. The LORD answered his prayer, and she became pregnant. Because there was so much activity going on in her womb while she was carrying her babies, she prayed and asked the LORD what was happening to her. Verse 23 says **"The LORD said to her, 'Two nations are in your womb, and two peoples from within you will be separated; one people will be stronger than the other, and the older will serve the younger (NIV).'"**

Rebekah gave birth to twin boys. The first baby born was red and hairy. He was so hairy until he looked like a garment. They named him Esau. The second one born was holding on to the first baby's heel with his hand; they named him Jacob. Before birth her sons were at odds with each other, because they wrestled against each other in her womb. Esau the first born grew to be a man that loved the open country; he liked to hunt and became very good at it. The Bible describes Jacob as a very quiet man that loved staying around the house. But, because Isaac loved to eat the wild games, he loved Esau, and because of prophecy Rebekah helped Jacob. The impact of their love for their sons was shown later on in their lives.

Esau's name meant red, because when he was born he was red. Jacob's name meant one who deceives, because when he was born he was holding on to his brother's heel. One day Esau came home from being out in the open field, probably hunting or exploring, and he was very hungry until the point of passing out. Jacob was cooking stew, and Esau asked for some. Jacob in turn told him that he would give him some if he would sell him his birthright. Esau replied, what good is a birthright to a man who is dead, because if he did not get anything to eat, he was going to die anyway? So, he agreed that Jacob could have his birthright. Then Jacob fed him. The Bible says that Esau despised his birthright. In other words, his birthright did not mean very much to him, because he sold it for a bowl of stew.

Funny that Jacob's name meant one who deceives, because he deceived his brother into verbally handing over his place as first born to him. Therefore, all of the blessings the first born that Esau was supposed to get had been given to Jacob. Perhaps, Esau really did not know what he had done. He certainly did not value his birthright from the looks of the deal.

After the incident of Esau trading in his birthright, Rebekah was faced with the same situation that God had protected Sarah from. A famine was in the land; therefore, Isaac had to move to Gerar where Abimelech, king of the Philistines was living. He too told the king that Rebekah was his sister instead of his wife, because she was so beautiful. He feared for his life. But, the king saw him hugging his wife, and had him brought to him. The king asked the same question that Abraham had been asked, why you told me that she is your sister when she is your wife. He said to Isaac that he could have brought guilt on them if anyone had slept with Rebekah. Of course, Isaac explained that he was afraid that he would be killed and his wife taken for someone else. The king gave orders that no one was to molest Isaac or Rebekah. Then Isaac and Rebekah lived in Gerar for a long time, and God blessed them in time of famine. In fact, they became so blessed and wealthy that the Philistines got jealous of them, and Abimelech told them that they had to move to another land.

When Esau was forty years old, he married two Canaanites women which displeased his parents. Isaac had grown very old and apparently had lost his eye sight. He realized that his life was coming near to the end. So, he told his son Esau to go to the open country, kill him some meat and prepare it for him to eat. Then he would bless him before his death. Esau went to do what his father had asked him to do. But, Rebekah heard what Isaac said to Esau. Because she knew the fate of her sons that was spoken to her by God while they were wresting in her womb, she was driven to intervene. I believe that at this point Rebekah had to devise and execute a plan to make sure that the spoken word from God to her was fulfilled. She was driven and determined to see the prophecy come to pass. So, she devised a plan that would guarantee Jacob getting the blessing that God had said that he would get.

Rebekah told Jacob to go and get her two of the best young goats so that she could prepare them for Isaac to eat. She gave Jacob some of Esau's clothes to put on, and she put some of the goats' hair on his hand and neck, so Isaac would think that it was Esau that he was talking to instead of Jacob. After she cooked the food just like Isaac liked it, she sent Jacob in with it to his father to receive Isaac's blessing. Although Isaac kept saying that the voice was Jacob, he concluded that he was talking to Esau because of the goats' hair on Jacob that he felt and the smell of Esau's clothes that Jacob was wearing. Therefore, Isaac blessed Jacob with the first born blessing. God and Rebekah's mission had been accomplished, because part of the blessing was that Jacob's brother would serve him.

When Esau returned home with the meat that he had gone out and killed for his father, he prepared it the way his father liked it and took it in to him. His father was shock and told him that he had blessed his brother, because he thought that he was talking to him. Jacob had deceived him. Evidently, after Isaac had spoken the blessing over Jacob; he could not take it back. Esau was terribly disappointed and became very angry with Jacob. He was so angry until he said that he would kill Jacob after the days of mourning for their father were over. When Rebekah was told what Esau was contemplating in his heart against Jacob, she came up with a plan to get Jacob away from Esau, because she did not want to lose both her sons. So, she told Jacob that he must leave and go to her brother for a while until his brother got over his anger for him. She went to Isaac and told him that Esau's wives really made her ill, and she could not live with the fact that Jacob may marry a Hittite woman too. So, Isaac called for Jacob, blessed him, and told him to go live with his mother's brother's family and take a wife from among his uncle's family. Jacob set off to live with his uncle, and the Bible does not talk about Rebekah again.

Rebekah's life reflects a woman who God used to make sure that his plans for Jacob would be fulfilled. If Isaac heard the words that God spoke about his sons, he was not going to obey them. He was on the course of doing things the traditional way which meant that the first born would get the greater blessing. Apparently, he never thought twice about what God's plans were for his sons, neither did he ask God what his plans were. He went about his merry way doing things his way, because he loved Esau more. Esau evidently appeared to be manlier than Jacob. But, Esau was not God's choice as to who would get the greater blessing and be named with the Fathers; Abraham, Isaac, and Jacob.

It is important to recognize that Rebekah loved Jacob, and it is obvious that she was the one to pour into Jacob's life, because Jacob spent quality time with his mother. We can see some of Rebekah's qualities in Jacob as we see him serve his uncle for years. Rebekah's goal in life after her sons' birth was to see to it that both her sons were reared in love, but also to see that Jacob was in the place that he needed to be for God's use. On the other hand, Jacob listened and obeyed his mother, because if he had not obeyed her, the plan would not have worked. Also, we see Esau 's disobedience and non-compliance with his parents in the fact that he took two wives from the Canaanites instead of staying with the custom of his father by marrying someone from his own family. Esau tried to obtain ratification for his disobedience from his parents by taking a wife from Ishmael's descendants after he learned that Isaac sent Jacob to find a wife from Rebekah's family. By saying that Isaac loved Esau and Rebekah loved Jacob does not mean that both boys were not loved by both of their parents. Their parents felt that one would be more successful than the other. Isaac looked at outward physical gifting, and Rebekah held on to the spoken word by God. Because Rebekah had a Rhema Word from God, she acted according to it.

The story of Rebekah and her sons lets us know that we can know the plans that God has for our children if we ask Him. As Christian mothers, we certainly want for our children what God want for them, and we should not make too many decisions concerning them based on our feelings or even their feelings without consulting God. Since everyone was created by God, everyone should seek to know the purpose in which He created them. This applies to adults as well as their children.

Rebekah's story also depicts a woman who was very humble and serving. These qualities were seen in her the first time we saw her when she gave Abraham's servants and their camels water. She loved her husband and sons very much, but she loved God more, because she risked her relationship with her husband and her oldest son in order to see that God's Word was fulfilled in their lives. She was forced to send Jacob away in order to save his life from his brother's wrath which probably meant that her relationship with Jacob became a very distant one. There was probably very little communication between them. The Bible does not really tell us whether or not Jacob saw his mother alive again after he left. We can almost conclude that her relationship with Jacob was completely cut off. The Bible does not tell us whether or not she had anymore contact with Jacob nor does it tell us when she died, because after Jacob went off to live with his uncle's family, she is not mentioned again.

Lastly, Rebekah was a strong-willed, courageous, and intelligent woman who knew how to plan and manipulate matters so that the matters would work according to God's purpose for her family. The Bible is very clear when it says that Isaac loved Rebekah. Because Rebekah was Isaac's help meet, she saw to it that he operated in righteousness by blessing the right son. Perhaps, she kept Isaac from the wrath of God. I am sure that after Isaac discovered that he had blessed Jacob instead of Esau, Rebekah explained to him why she did what she did. Rebekah probably had to remind him of God's spoken word after he blessed Jacob. However, she must have known that the blessing had to come first, because she knew that her husband was going to do things his way. Notice when it was time for Jacob to leave, she went to her husband and talked to him about Jacob marrying a Hittite woman who would have been very perplexing and grievous to them. Esau had already put a bad taste in their mouth by marrying women outside of their family, because it was not customary for them to marry outside of their own kin. Isaac told Jacob to go to his mother's father's family and take a wife from them, and he blessed him. Jacob set off with the blessing of his father. So, Rebekah made Isaac think that it was his idea to send Jacob away.

In conclusion, Isaac and Rebekah was the only couple in the first fathers that was married only to each other. Abraham and Jacob had other wives and maidservants but not Isaac. Therefore, Rebekah never had to compete with another woman for her husband. Her husband truly loved her and kept her as his only wife. That's a testimony within itself. We never see them openly disagree; although there was a disagreement in who should get the greater blessing. Although, Rebekah appeared to favor one son over the other, she loved both her sons. She saw to it that Jacob went away until Esau cooled down, because it would have been devastating to have one of her sons killing the other. Esau would have lived in shame and misery from that day forward. Besides, Rebekah knew God's plan for her boys, and she was confident in what she did. Being the strong godly woman that she was, Rebekah saw to it that God's Word was fulfilled in her sons' lives.

Chapter 4

Leah and Rachel

In Genesis 29, Jacob arrived at his mother's homeland, and he asked some men how to find his Uncle Laban. They pointed out to him Laban's daughter, Rachel, who was approaching them with her father's sheep. She was coming to let the sheep drink water from a well that had a stone in front of it. She was called a shepherdess, because she attended to the sheep. Jacob greeted her with a hug and kiss; then he told her that he was her aunt Rebekah's son. This time, Jacob went looking for a woman, one who would be pleasing to God, his parents, and to himself. He loved and wanted Rachel from the first time he saw her. When her father asked what he could do for him, Jacob told him that he would work for him for seven years if he would give Rachel to be his wife; Laban agreed.

But after the seven years passed, the night that Jacob was to consummate his marriage, Laban sent Leah into his tent instead of Rachel. Jacob woke up the next morning with Leah in his arms and not Rachel. I can't imagine what he must have felt, but he must have learned from this experience what Esau felt when he learned that he (Jacob) had gotten his blessing. In other words, he realized that he had been deceived just as he had deceived his father and his brother. Jacob went to Laban and asked why he had tricked him. Laban told him that it was not their custom to give the younger daughter in marriage before the oldest is given. So, Laban told Jacob to finish out the week with Leah, and then he would give Rachel to him for another seven years of labor. Jacob agreed to do what Laban asked him to do, and Rachel became his wife after his first week with Leah. Although, Laban gave Rachel to Jacob early; Jacob was still indebted to him for seven years.

Needless to say there were much conflict between Leah and Rachel. The Bible describes Leah as weak eyes or perhaps crossed-eyes. Her description tells us that she must not have been very attracted looking to Jacob. Because her father probably thought that she was not very appealing to men, he tricked Jacob into marrying her. But Rachel was beautiful and lovely in form; everything about her was pleasing to Jacob. Jacob loved Rachel more than Leah. Because God saw that Leah was not loved, He opened her womb and closed Rachel's womb for a season. Leah had four sons before she stopped having babies for a while. Each time she had a son, she would say surely my husband will love me now. In the meantime, Rachel became jealous and gave her maidservant, Bilhah to Jacob to have a son which would be raised as her own. After Bilhah was given to Jacob as a wife, he slept with her, and she bore him two sons. Rachel named both of her sons and said to herself that the LORD had vindicated her because her struggle with her sister had been great. Then, she felt better about herself. To get back at Rachel, Leah in turn gave Jacob her maidservant, Zilpah, and she bore him two sons also that Leah named. There was a great struggle between these two sisters to please or gain more attention from their husband. The competition was strong, but Leah still recognized that Jacob loved Rachel more. Evidently, Jacob spent most of his nights with Rachel, because when Leah's oldest son found some mandrakes, Rachel asked Leah for some of her son's mandrakes. Leah's reply was that she had already taken away her husband and that she wanted to take her son's mandrakes too. Rachel told Leah that she would let Jacob be with her that night in return for her son's mandrakes. When Jacob came home that evening, Leah ran out to him and told him that she had hired him for the night. He slept with her, and she became pregnant. Leah had two more sons and said that now her husband would honor her, because she had borne him six sons, and later Leah had a girl. Then God remembered Rachel, and she gave birth to Joseph. Rachel gave birth to her second son and Jacob's twelfth son, and then she died shortly after her son's Benjamin's birth.

Leah's conflict and competition for her husband ended with Rachel's death, and there were no mention of any conflicts that she had with Bilhah and Zilpah, the maidservants. Leah became Jacob's primary or main wife if I am allowed to say it that way. She became the mother of all the children especially Rachel's. She was the only mother that Benjamin the baby boy knew. It's amazing how God vindicates us sometimes. The Bible makes clear that Jacob loved Rachel, but the Bible never said that Jacob loved Leah too nor does it say that Jacob loved Rachel more than Leah. Leah struggled with the fact that her husband loved and desired to be with her sister to the point that she was extremely neglected by him. She really believed that by her having sons for her husband that it would make him desire her more, and he probably did to a certain degree. But, love is all about a choice. This is why God is specific in the law about marriage. You cannot love two people equally, and three people cannot become one. This story paints a clear picture of the cliché that 'Two is company and three is a crowd.' Also, you cannot serve two masters; you will love one and hate the other. We know that this Scripture is talking about money and God, but it can also apply to the faithfulness of spouses to their mates. Mates are supposed to serve each other by fulfilling their marital needs. Evidently, Leah was not fulfilled while Rachel was there.

God used Leah in spite of the fact that she was second to her younger sister Rachel in Jacob's heart. God saw that Leah was not loved; therefore he blessed her to give birth to six sons. Our God is so compassionate and loving. He sent comfort to Leah in the form of precious babies. He showed her favor over Rachel by allowing her to have all of her babies before Rachel ever had one. This was God's way of saying to Jacob that Leah was precious and deserved to be loved too. Evidently, Jacob was pleased to continue to sleep with her if for only to continue having children.

When Rachel gave birth to her first child, she named him Joseph and said, **"God has taken away my disgrace (Genesis 30:23, NIV)."** Rachel's son Joseph was an awesome man of God whom the LORD used mightily. The Bible says that God's favor was with him and that God cause him to find favor with men wherever he was even during the time when he was in prison; the guards showed him favor. God used him by allowing him to interpret dreams to become second to the pharaoh in his time, and through the knowledge that God gave him, he saved the world from starvation. Because God visited him in dreams as a young child, he already knew that he had the favor of God in his life. Joseph was Rachel's oldest son.

Although, God used Joseph in a mighty way, he did not leave Leah's son out when it came to giving out anointing. We really do not know how old Joseph was when Rachel died. We can only assume that he was still very young. Since he was very young, Leah ended up rearing him as her own. Because Jacob loved him more than his other sons, they were jealous of him and sold him as a slave to foreigners. His brothers thought he was arrogant and spoiled rotten. They probably had a valid argument since their father made him a coat of many colors and made them nothing. God allowed him to go through many tests by being enslaved and in prison, but Joseph came out on top. One can assume that the development of his character came from his rearing from Jacob and Leah. So, in a sense, we can assume that Joseph's humbleness when dealing with the men he served as a servant in Potipher's house, a prisoner, and Pharoah's right-hand man came from the influenced of his mother Leah and father Jacob. His character and attitude about God cause him to have favor with God and man. These are qualities that one should be reared up to have but can be trained to have too. Joseph was Rachel's biological son, but Leah was the mother he grew up under and knew.

Later on, God used Leah's son Levi's descendants as the family of priests that were the only ones allowed to come into his temple to offer sacrifices to him. When Leah had Levi, she said, **"'Now at last my husband will become attached to me, because I have borne him three sons.' So he was named Levi (Genesis 29:34, NIV)."** Every time Leah had a son, she named him according to what she was feeling or how God was ministering to her at the time. She used the word attached to connect to the name Levi. Since Levi's name had something to do with attaching, God used his blood line, because the attachment to Him (God) would be because of affection and loyalty. God needs and wants his priests to be bonded to him by ties of affection and loyalty. The priests of God spent their lives dedicated to God and God's service. Levi was Leah's third baby. The fact that Levi was the number three son can also be parallel with the trinity: the father, the Son, and the Holy Spirit. The next step down from the trinity would be man; not just any man but an attached man to God needed to be in place, a priest, one given only to render himself to God.

God also used Leah's son Judah's descendants as the family of the praise and worshippers to minister praise and worship unto him. When Leah gave birth to Judah, she said, **"This time I will praise the LORD (Genesis 29:35, NIV)."** Judah's name meant praise. Ironically, Judah was the fourth son; therefore, he came after the priest to be the worshipper. So, it is fitting that he would be the tribe in which God called to be the ones to give God praise. Jesus is often called the Lion of the Tribe of Judah, because Jesus was born through the blood line of Judah. (See Matthew 1:2&3) Jacob spoke his destiny or place in God's kingdom work on earth when he blessed his sons before he died. Jacob called him praise too. As a matter of fact, Jacob prophesied that Jesus would come through his blood line in Genesis, Chapter 49: 8-12.

It is plain to see that Leah and Rachel had a relationship with God, because they both communed with him and gave him credit each time they borne children or their maidservants borne children. The Scriptures also plainly show that God was with them and granted their requests at various times. Even before Leah asked, God saw that she was not loved. He opened her wound in order for her to gain a little love from her husband. I believe that God did not open Rachel's wound until he saw to it that Jacob showed Leah some respect and love. After all, who would not have a little love for someone they spent so much time sleeping with and having babies with. If we refer back to Genesis 30:20, Leah said, **"God has presented me with a precious gift. This time my husband will treat me with honor, because I have borne him six sons (NIV)."** From that time on, Jacob probably treated her with honor, because after then, God opened Rachel's womb, and she had two sons.

It was sad that two sisters had to compete and be at odds with each other for the same husband, but God did not allow them to grow old dealing with the turmoil. After Rachel's death, Leah was left as Jacob's only wife. What I love about Leah is that she recognized that there was a God and that all of her help came from Him. Rachel on the other hand ended up taking an image that her father held as one of his gods which was the demised of her death. But, Leah served her husband's God and trusted him, because she had developed a serious relationship with God during the course of her struggles with her sister and during the birth of her seven children. Also, needless to say the rearing of her children and the fact that her husband loved her sister more than he loved her were struggles that she had to endure. But, Leah gave God credit and honor for showing her favor and love in what may have seemed like over her sister, because she was favored to give Jacob sons, and Rachel was not for a while. Leah lived with Jacob many years after Rachel's death. Although the Bible does not clearly say when she died we assume that she reared Rachel's baby, Benjamin to be a grown-up before she died. We do know that she was still living when Joseph was sold by his brothers, because Joseph told his father and mother about a dream that he had which got him sold into slavery shortly after.

Leah attached destiny to her sons when she named them. She praised God in the midst of her struggles. God allowed her to be triumphant in the end. As I stated earlier, only two can become one in a marriage not three. Leah had her husband to herself, and Jacob honored her as the mother of all of his children. We can see this in Genesis 37:10 when he rebuked Joseph for saying that he and his mother would bow to him (Joseph). Jacob honored Leah when he buried her in the field and cave where his fathers and mothers were buried: Abraham, Sarah, Isaac, and Rebekah (Genesis 49:31). Yes, just as Leah spoke after the birth of her last son, **"Now my husband will honor me, because I have borne him six sons (Genesis 30:20, NIV),"** Jacob did honor her even above Rachel with this act. Rachel was not buried where Jacob and Leah would later be buried. God saw to it that Leah was indeed honored.

Chapter 5

Pioneer Women of God

Shiphrah and Puah

In the Book of Exodus in the first Chapter, we find a very short story about two very brave women, Shiphrah and Puah. They were Hebrew midwives in Egypt under the Pharoah's reign. At that time the Israelites had become the Egyptian's slaves. After Pharoah saw that the Israelites had become great in number and were continually increasing, he became concerned that the Israelites might team up with another nation who would come against Egypt and take over his kingdom. He called for Shiphrah and Puah, and ordered them to kill every boy that they would help to deliver, but they were told to let every girl live. Because Shiphrah and Puah feared God, they would not carry out the Pharoah's plan. In other words the midwives feared and respected God over the Pharoah; they risked their lives, because they obeyed God rather than man. Pharoah had the power and authority according to man's law to put them to death for disobeying him. These women did a very courageous and heroic thing when they refused to put the babies to death. They got God's attention. Granted, they lied to the Pharoah to turn his anger away from them by telling him that the Hebrew women were not like the Egyptian women. The Hebrew women were stronger, because they would have already given birth before they could arrive at their homes. But, because Shiphrah and Puah feared God, God blessed them and gave them families of their own. These were women who dared not to go against God, and God favored them (Exodus 1:15-21).

Moses' Mother

In the second chapter of the Book of Exodus, the Bible introduces us to Moses by telling of his birth and the circumstances surrounding it. With the hardships of the heavy, harsh labor that was put on the Israelites and the execution law of the baby boys to be killed, God had to send someone to deliver the Israelites from the powerful Egyptians. The deliverer had to come from within the Israelites nation. Since Shiphrah and Puah would not kill the Hebrew baby boys, the Egyptians did; therefore, God used a woman to execute a plan in order to get a deliverer in their midst. The Bible only calls her Moses' mother a woman from the tribe of Levi; her name is not mentioned in the chapter that tells of Moses' birth at all. Later, in Exodus 6: 20, her name, Jochebed, appears in the family record or ancestors of Moses. When Moses's mother gave birth to him, she saw that he was beautiful. She even saw something very special in him. Maybe, the special thing that she saw in him was just simply, he was her baby; but never the less she felt that he had to be saved. So, she hid him for three months. When she felt that she could no longer hide him, she had to develop a plan to save him from the Egyptians. Moses' mother took a basket made of papyrus reed and sealed it with tar and pitch (a dark, sticky substance obtained from coal tar, etc. used for waterproofing according to Webster's II Dictionary) to keep water from getting into it. The Bible says that she covered it all over or coated it to make sure that it was perfectly sealed. Then she placed her baby in the basket and carefully put it among the reeds along the bank of the Nile River.

Undoubtedly, Moses' mother must have known that the Pharoah's daughter came to the Nile to take a bath each day. So, she had the basket with the baby in it in place when Pharoah's daughter arrived for her bath that day. But, Jochebed, Moses' mother did not just leave the baby for Pharoah's daughter to find it, she sent her daughter to see what would happen when the Pharoah's daughter discovered him. Moses' mother appealed to the compassionate heart of a woman by putting a beautiful baby in front of her to decide his fate. I am sure that because the baby was beautiful, it made it even harder for the Pharoah's daughter to say, kill him or give him over to be killed. When Pharoah's daughter saw the baby, she had compassion and decided to raise him as her own. Moses' sister was watching as she drew him out of the Nile. She saw Pharoah's daughter express compassion. Moses' sister immediately ran up to Pharoah's daughter and asked her to let her call one of the Hebrew mothers to nurse and take care of him until he was weaned; Pharoah's daughter agreed.

Of course, the sister called her mother to nurse the baby. The Pharoah's daughter gave the baby to his mother and told her that she would pay her for taking care of him. So, the baby was given back to his mother to care for him until he was weaned. LOOK AT GOD! Not only did his mother get to take care of him for a little while longer, but she was also paid to do it by Pharoah's daughter. WHAT AN AWESOME GOD! After the baby grew and was weaned, Moses' mother gave him back to Pharoah's daughter to rear as her son.

Like it would hurt any mother to give up her baby, I am sure that it hurt Moses' mother to give him up to be reared as someone else's son. But, she knew that it was better to give him up to someone else in order to save his life than to hold on to him; until someone discovered that she had him. If he had been discovered by any of the other Egyptians, he would have been taken from her and killed. I believe that God orchestrates people's lives so that we really see God working his plans through people not them working their own plans. This was the case of Moses' mother. Her role was just to be obedient to God's will and plan for her life and her children's lives, because not only did God use Moses mightily, he also used two more of her children mightily, Miriam and Aaron. Miriam is seen later on in the Scripture, and Aaron was the High Priest. Out of all the Levite women, God chose her. Since God is the only one that knows the heart, He knew that she was the willing vessel that would do what He needed her to do. So, we see another brave and courageous woman that dared to defy man's rule and that was obedience to God's commands which brought forward a deliverer that God used to bring deliverance to her people, the Israelites. Jochebed, Moses's mother, was an awesome woman of God.

Miriam

We assume that the girl who was Moses's sister that kept watch over the baby in the basket after being placed in the Nile River among the reeds by his mother was Miriam, because she is the only sister that the Bible talks about. God used her as a part of his plan to keep Moses alive. Even Miriam showed courage when she stepped up and asked the Pharoah's daughter should she call a Hebrew woman to care for the baby. After the Pharoah's daughter gave her consent to call a Hebrew woman, she brought her mother, which was the baby's mother also, to her to care for him. Because, she followed God's plan, she was also very instrumental in the fate of Moses and her people as a young girl.

We did not see Miriam again until Moses and Aaron led the Israelites out of Egypt. After they crossed over the Red Sea on dry land with the Egyptians in hot pursuit behind them, the LORD brought the sea back to normal. The Egyptians were drowned. Moses sang a victory song. Then the Bible says that Miriam, the prophetess, took a tambourine and led the women in song. As Moses sang, they answered him (Exodus 15:20). By leading the women in song, she showed the qualities of a leader too. Miriam was called a prophetess in this passage of Scripture; therefore, she had to have been used by God to exhort, to edify and to comfort others (I Corinthians 14:3). Also, due to some history of leadership and ability, it seemed that the women had no problems following her in song.

The last time we see Miriam is in the Book of Numbers. This time Miriam stepped outside of her boundaries with God. Numbers 12:1 says, **"And Miriam and Aaron spake against Moses because of the Ethiopian woman whom he had married: for he had married an Ethiopian woman (KJV)."** They got attention in a negative way and caused God to become very angry with them for ridiculing Moses because of who he married or his wife. Apparently, she did not meet the standards in which they thought she should have. She was from another nation of people. Evidently, they must have thought that they were equal to Moses in the assignments that God had given for them to do, because God told them that he would speak to Moses directly and give instructions to him not them. After God rebuked Aaron and Miriam, he departed from them in a cloud. Miriam became leprous immediately, Aaron begged for forgiveness and Moses begged God to heal her. In order to teach Miriam and Aaron a valuable lesson, God let her remain leprous for seven days living outside the camp. In other words, God just put her on punishment for seven days, and she was received back into the camp after the seven days were over. The Israelites did not move until she was allowed back into the camp. We do not see Miriam anymore after this incident. We can only assume that she was taught a lesson that would cause her never to have to be corrected by God again. Nevertheless, Miriam was a woman who was mightily used by God and who was obedience to God's Will for her life.

Zipporah

Zipporah was introduced in Exodus 2: 21 as the daughter of the priest of Midian who he gave to Moses to be his wife. There was not much written about her, but she too played an important part in saving Moses's life once. Exodus 4:24-26 paints a picture of God being angry at Moses for not doing what He had asked him to do. The time came when God told Moses to go back to Egypt and tell the Pharoah to let his people go. During Moses' journey back to Egypt, he stopped at an inn for the night along with his wife and son. The LORD met Moses there and was going to kill him. But, Zipporah circumcised their son: therefore, God did not kill Moses.

Part of God's covenant with the Israelites beginning with Abraham, Isaac, and Jacob was that all males were to be circumcised. Apparently, since Moses had not grown up with the Israelites nor was his wife an Israelite, they did not deem it important to practice the customs of the Israelites. But God did, because God deals in Excellency. One must adhere to and follow the rules that He set for them. Besides, how could Moses claim to be one of the Israelites and not practice their customs or be in covenant with God, because this was a covenant requirement? This would have been a tool that the enemy could have used against Moses' leadership. God must have informed Moses that he needed to circumcise his son, and evidently, Zipporah must have known what was being required too. She also knew that God was getting ready to kill Moses in order for her to react the way that she did. By her performing the circumcision on her son, Moses' life was spared.

Since the Bible never says that Moses had another wife, we assumed that Zipporah was his only wife. The Bible does not record anymore of her actions, but she was talked about later when Aaron and Miriam criticized Moses because of his wife. As stated earlier, this story is found in the Book of Numbers, the twelfth chapter. The King James Bible Version identifies her as an Ethiopian woman, but the New International Bible Version identifies her as a Cushite woman which could mean the same. The point is that she was not an Israelite; therefore, Aaron and Miriam thought it was a valid reason to disqualify Moses as the set man of God. They must have felt that Moses did not meet all of God standards after all he had taken a wife from outside of their nation. But, God quickly put a stop to their criticisms of Moses and his wife.

In today's world, there are countless men and women of God who are unhappy and getting divorces because of the people under their leadership who feel that they have somehow been given the right to criticize their leadership by criticizing their spouses. They surround themselves with other people, innocent people, and plant words and ideas into their minds and hearts to make leadership look invalid because of the way his wife or her husband acts. In most cases they talk against men and especially women, pastor's wives to be exact because of who they are and what they represent to the body of Christ. These people seem to be very skillful in their ability to manipulate people and now more than usual to manipulate leaders into thinking that their spouses are all wrong for the ministry and eventually wrong for them. Men are replacing their wives with church members due to how many church members who are opposed to their wives. Satan has placed people in cliques in churches just to destroy the men of God family units; therefore, alternately destroying their creditability and ministry.

Today, men are not waiting on the LORD to deal with such people; they do not consult God at all. They listen to people complaints about their spouses which they should not have in the first place and let them plant evil thoughts in their minds concerning their spouses; until they become evil toward their spouses. They do not let God deal with the evilness in people just as he dealt with it with the case of Aaron and Miriam. They allow people to remain evil and to keep on dividing and conquering families for Satan's glory. They first become Satan's prey not knowing and after he has devoured them from God's use, they become his servants but think that they are God's leaders. They do not think for one minute that they are ruled by the evil people who they have surrounded themselves with, because the people are who control their thoughts about other people. There are several stories in the Bible that depicts men and women planting evil thoughts in kings' minds and causes them to get rid of their spouses and sometimes other people. For example, Queen Esther and the queen before her were victims of this situation.

The ugly end of what Satan planned for Zipporah's demised did not work. God immediately stepped in and stopped the madness that Aaron and Miriam had allowed themselves to enter into. Thank God for when He dealt with them, they did not allow their hearts to become harder. They recognized that God was serious and that He was not going to put up with their foolishness, and they all repented immediately. They probably had a beautiful, loving relationship with Zipporah from that day forward, because God unquestionably made them aware that He was not pleased with them talking about her. It is not wise for people to open their mouths against the women of God that God has in place as a help meet to the men of God in leadership.

Chapter 6

Women of War

It is extremely important to note that God is not a respecter of persons (Acts 10:34, KJV) and that God uses whomever he wants to fulfill his plans in the earth. It is also important for men and women to know that God calls them for a specific purpose, and they should be ready and willing to walk in it when God says to do so. As the next several women are introduced, we will see them used by God in times of war and/or as governmental officials.

Rahab

After Moses died, the Lord told Joshua that it was time to lead the people into the promise land. They were to go in and take possession of several cities. Judges 2 depicts a woman who was brave enough to take a stand against her people and aide the two Israelites who had come into her city to spy out the land. Joshua sent the two men secretly to explore the land in the area in which God was giving them as the promise land. He told them to pay close attention especially to the city of Jericho. After they entered the city of Jericho, they went into a prostitute's house, her name was Rahab. Someone told the king of Jericho that two Israelites had entered their city and had gone into Rahab's house. The king ordered Rahab to bring the men out, because they had come into their city to spy out the land and to look for the best way to come into the city to attack it. But, Rahab told the king's men that she did not know that the men were spies and that they had left just before the city's gates were closed. She said that she did not know where they were going, but if they would hurry and go after them, they probably had time to catch up to them. The king's men left the city in pursuit of the two spies.

Jericho must have been located in an area that made it almost impossible for people to come in and out of it without being noticed or seen. One thing that aided the city in their protection was its position near the Jordan River. When the king's men left in pursuit of the spies, they were careful to check all the low or shallow places of the river in which the spies might have crossed. Evidently, they could not get back to their people without crossing the Jordan River. Also, the city had a very serious wall built all the way around it, and everyone had to enter and exit through gates.

Rahab had hidden the two spies on top of her roof under some flax poles. Before they went to sleep that night, she talked to them about their God. She told them that her whole city was fearful of them, because they had heard about what God did to the Egyptians in the Red Sea after he led the Israelites through it on dry ground. She also told them that they had heard about how God caused them to totally destroy the two kings, Sihon and Og and their people. Everyone in their city was afraid of them, because they recognized that their God was to be feared above all gods. Further, Rahab told them that she knew that God was giving them that land; therefore, she wanted to make a deal with them. She asked them to show her and her family kindness when they come in to take the land just as she had shown them kindness by not turning them over to her king. In other words, she said that since I have saved your lives, promise me that you will save my family and me. Rahab asked them to save her father and mother and all that belonged to their household. The two men agreed to return the kindness. They told her that if she did not tell what they were doing there, they would see to it that her house would be saved. But, she must have all of her family members inside her house when they come to take the city and none of them must not leave out and go into the street, because if they did, then they would not be held accountable for their lives.

Because Rahab's house was a part of the city wall, she let the men climb down on the outer part of the city by a red or scarlet rope. She told them to go into the hill and stay there until three days, because the men who had gone out to pursue them will have returned, and then they could get away safely. The men told her to make sure that she kept the rope hanging from her house, so their people would be able to identify her house. Also, they reminded her that if she broke her promise, then they would not honor their agreement. They went into the hills, and after three days returned to Joshua to report to him all that happened.

In Joshua 6:17, the fate of Rahab is revealed. God caused the walls of Jericho to fall down. The Israelites went in and killed all the men, women, children and animals except the ones in Rahab's house just as the spies promised her. Joshua told the spies to go into Rahab's house and bring her and everyone in her family out into safety. They went in and brought out Rahab, her father, mother, brothers and all the others who were there as part of her family. They brought them out and placed them in a place outside the Israelites' camp; the Bible says that they still live among the Israelites today. Then, the Israelites burned the whole city down to the ground after taking the gold, silver, bronze, and iron for the treasury in the Lord's house. Joshua spoke a curse on anyone who would attempt to rebuild the city of Jericho again.

Because Rahab believed in the Israelites' God and risked her life to protect and save the two spies that Joshua sent to spy out her city, God spared not only her but her whole family. He kept them from being destroyed when everyone and everything else around them were totally annihilated. Rahab gained favor when she stood up for God's people, and that favor caused her to be counted among God's people, because she is named in Matthew 1: 5 in the genealogy of Jesus. Although, Rahab was called a prostitute, she understood when it was time to put foolishness and sin aside and to catch onto the plan of God.

By listening to the stories that were told of the miracles performed for the Israelites, Rahab's mind was enlightened, and she found an everlasting God that would never go back on his promises. What Rahab experienced was two-folds. She not only was saved physically, but spiritually too. Rahab left a people and a world that allowed her to be a prostitute, and she joined a people and a world that would not allow her to even think about sins. I am sure that she felt as most prostitutes do: trapped, de-valued, dirty, and ashamed of her way of living. Rahab caught a glimpse of what freedom and redemption looked like, and she wanted it for herself. She wanted to be cleaned and unashamed. She wanted to be who she really was, and she knew that if she could get God's attention, he would help her. In other words, she left an unrighteous life style and an unrighteous people. As a matter of fact, she watched God completely destroy the world and all the unrighteous people in it that she had known all of her life. He destroyed all of her possessions and even her house of sin. But, she was pleased to take part in helping to aide God's people in doing so, because she came out with something much more valuable than she could ever imagine. Rahab gained the favor of God and was given the privilege to live a righteous life. After the destruction of Jericho, she did not have to be reminded of her sinful life, because all the people that she had been with and the place where she did her business were no more. She buried her past of unrighteousness and sins and joined into righteousness. Rahab was given a new life. She could now have a husband who would respect her for being a God fearing woman. Her husband would never have to encounter another man that she had been engaged in sin with, because they had been destroyed. She was someone to be proud of instead of being ashamed of.

Rahab did not just think about herself when she asked to be saved, unselfishly, she asked that her whole family would be saved, and she saw to it that they were in the right place at the right time. When the Israelites went in to bring her out safely, her family came out with her. Now, Rahab is accredited for the salvation of her entire family. All of them were given the gift of life physically and spiritually, everlasting life, because from that day forward they became God's people. Rahab received beauty for ashes, because she did a beautiful thing. So, she had to be happy as a woman who was found worthy to be a part of God's family. What a wonderful way to end up!

Deborah

The story of Deborah is found in Judges 4 and 5. The Israelites had done evil in the Lord's eyes. So, God sold them into the hands of a Canaanite king, named Jabin. Sisera was the commander of Jabin's army. Because Sisera had a large army and nine hundred iron chariots, he treated the Israelites cruelly for twenty years. But, the Israelites knew God as a deliverer. After all, they were the people that God delivered from Egypt. So, the Israelites cried out to God for help.

At that time, the Israelites were being led by a woman named Deborah. The Bible calls her a prophetess and a judge. Her husband's name was Lappidoth. She held court under the Palm of Deborah between Ramah and Bethel in the country of Ephraim. Deborah made the judgments in all of the Israelites' disputes that were brought to her.

One day she sent for a man name Barak from the tribe of Naphtali and said to him, **"The LORD, the God of Israel, commands you: 'Go, take with you ten thousand men of Naphtali and Zebulun and lead the way to Mount Tabor. I will lure Sisera, the commander of Jabin's army, with his chariots and his troops to the Kishon River and give him into your hands (Judges 4: 6-7, NIV).'"** But Barak refused to go unless she went with him. Deborah agreed to go with him, but told him that the LORD will hand Sisera over to a woman and that he would not get the honor. Barak gathered the ten thousand men from Zebulun and Naphtali, and they followed him along with Deborah.

As soon as Sisera heard that Barak had gathered an army and gone up to Mount Tabor, he gathered his army and nine hundred chariots from Harosheth Haggoyim to the Kishon River. Then Deborah told Barak to go because that was the day that God was going to give Sisera into his hands. She encouraged Barak by asking him, **"Has not the LORD gone ahead of you (Judges 4:14, NIV)?"** So, Barak and his men went down Mount Tabor, and the LORD routed Sisera, all of his chariots and all of his army by the sword. When the battle got too heated for Sisera, he abandoned his chariot and fled by foot. Barak pursued Sisera's chariots and army until every man in his army was killed by the sword.

Sisera ran to the tent of Jael, the wife of Heber the Kenite, because King Jabin and the clan of Heber the Kenite were friends. They had operated as friends in some of their affairs, but Heber and all of the Kenites were descendants of Moses' brother-in-law. However, Heber was not living in the land with the other Kenites, he had moved out from them. When Jael saw Sisera coming, she went out to meet him. She invited him into her tent and told him not be afraid. Jael gave Sisera some milk and placed covers over him so he could rest. Sisera told her to stand in the door and if anyone ask have she seen him to say no. Because he was exhausted from fighting and running, he went to sleep. While he was asleep, Jael picked up a tent peg, a hammer, and went quietly to where he was sleeping. She drove the peg through his temple all the way to the ground.

When Barak was coming by Jael's tent in pursuit of Sisera, she went out to meet him. She told him that she would show him the man that he was looking for. Jael took Barak into her tent and showed him Sisera lying dead with the peg through his temple. The same day, God subdued King Jabin before the Israelites. The Israelites grew stronger, and they totally destroyed Jabin, the Canaanite king. Then there was peace in the land for forty years.

The entire Fifth Chapter of Judges is the Song of Deborah. She and Barak sang the story of how God caused them to defeat King Jabin, Commander Sisera, and their army. Deborah sang of how God used her to judge and prophesy to the Israelites, because when Israel was in need of a leader, she arose as a mother to them. She sang about the heroic thing that Jael did by killing the evil commander, Sisera. Jael was called the most blessed of all tent-dwelling women. Deborah and Barak sang and celebrated the victory that God gave them. They sang about the treasures of the king and the commander that they were able to possess. They even sang about the other tribes that joined them and aided them in battle. Benjamin, Ephraim and Issachar fought along with them.

The story of Deborah is very clear about how God used a woman to lead the Israelites during that time. This story is an example of the Scripture that says God is no respecter of person. Man always portraits the woman as the one who is under the man. A woman should never be a leader over a man or usurp authority over a man is the Scripture found in I Timothy 2: 12 often quoted (KJV). But, God did not see it that way, because He used Deborah and made her the leader of all of the Israelites especially the men. God uses whoever He chooses and equips for the job. Evidently, Deborah was the one He equipped, because He used her mightily. He also used Jael to defeat Sisera. Prior, Deborah had prophesied to Barak that God would deliver Sisera into a woman's hand, because he would not go to war without her. God did just that! He caused Jael to be the one to kill Sisera, and she was and is still honored for her heroic act.

The story of Deborah should encourage any and every woman who has leadership edged into their spirit. If you know that God has called you to leadership whether in the body of Christ as ministers or in the corporate business world, then you should strive to obtain your ministry. You should also be aware that Satan will fight hard against you to keep you from accomplishing what God has called you to do. But, if Satan sees you as no threat or what you are doing as something that he has no need to worry about, then he will not bother you very much. Satan gets concern about those who will damage and destroy his kingdom. Leaders should be ready to go full speed ahead in spite of adversities.

Samson's Mother

The Israelites did evil in the eyes of the LORD again. This time the LORD gave them into the hands of the Philistines. The LORD allowed the Philistines to rule over them for forty years. When the LORD decided to do something about the Philistines, He looked for a woman to bring forth a judge and deliverer. God sent an angel to a married woman who was sterile and childless. The woman's husband was Manoah from the tribe of Dan. The Bible does not give her name, but an angel appeared to her and said, **"You are sterile and childless,**

but you are going to conceive and have a son. Now see to it that you drink no wine or other fermented drink and that you do not eat anything unclean, because you will conceive and give birth to a son. No razor may be used on his head, because the boy is to be a Nazarite, set apart to God from birth, and he will begin the deliverance of Israel from the hands of the Philistines (Judges 13: 3-5, NIV)."

The woman found her husband and told him all the things that the angel had told her. She also told him that the man who came to her looked very awesome, like an angel. The woman, Samson's mother told her husband that she did not ask the man where he came from, and the man did not tell her his name. Her husband prayed and begged the LORD to send the man of God to them again, so he could tell them or teach them how to rear the boy who was to be born. God heard his prayer, and He sent the angel of God to the woman again while she was out in the field. Her husband was not in the field with her, so she ran to get him. When she got to him, she told him that the man who had appeared to her was there. Manoah, her husband followed her to where the man was standing. Manoah asked the man was he the one who talked to his wife. The man answered, **"I am."**

Then Manoah asked the man to tell him what will be the rules for the boy's life. The man told him that his wife must do exactly what he commanded her to do. He gave Manoah all of the instructions that he had given his wife to do. Then the man said to Maonah again that his wife must do everything that he commanded her.

Manoah asked the angel of the LORD to stay and let them prepare food for him. The angel told him that he would not eat any food, but if he prepared a burnt offering, then he could offer it to the LORD. All of the time that Manoah had been talking to the man, he did not realize that the man was the angel of the LORD. When Manoah asked the man what was his name in order to honor him when the prophecy came to pass, the angel replied, **"Why do you ask my name? It is beyond understanding (Judges 13: 18, NIV)."**

Then Manoah sacrificed a young goat, along with a grain offering on a rock to the LORD. When the flame blazed up from the altar toward heaven, the angel of the LORD ascended in the flame while Manoah and his wife watched. They both quickly fell with their faces to the ground. After they did not see the man again, they realized that he was the angel of the LORD. Manoah thought that he had seen God and told his wife that they were **"doomed to die!"** His wife assured him by saying that if God meant to kill them, he would not have accepted their offerings nor showed them all the things that they saw or told them things to come. The woman gave birth to the boy that the angel of the LORD told her that she would have, and she named him Samson. The boy grew up to be very strong with God's spirit stirring him, because the LORD blessed him.

The story of Samson has been told many times and in many ways through verbal communication and visual communication, such as movies. Many children's books and plays are written about him, and there are many sermons that have been given across the pulpits in churches about him all over the world. Samson is probably thought to be the strongest man that ever lived; after all he fought and killed several giants at one time. But, this particular story is not directly focusing on Samson, it is about the woman who God gave the responsibility to bring Samson into the earth and rear him up according to God's Word that was spoken to her by the angel of the LORD. As I stated when I begin this story, when God decided to bring some deliverance to Israelites from the cruel Philistines, he first looked for and found a woman that would obey his commands.

The name of Samson's mother is not found in the Bible. She is only called a woman or Manoah's wife. But, it is ironic that God sent the angel of the LORD to her while she was not in the present of her husband twice. The angel spoke to her and told her that she was going to give birth to a son, but more importantly, he told her how to care for herself first while carrying the child. Then he instructed her to not let a razor touch the boy or in reality at that point in his life the man's head or any part of his body. The angel spoke Samson's purpose for coming into the earth to his mother. In essence, he gave her an awesome job to do; she had to make sure that she got her part right, and at the same time see to it that Samson obeyed her. Notice that God did not speak to Manoah about the boy until his wife took him to the angel of the LORD. It is clearly depicted that God did not ask for Manoah's agreement or permission to use his wife nor did He think twice about giving her direct orders while excluding him. When God chooses people for specific purposes He deals directly with them. The only reason that He sent the angel back to Manoah's wife is because Manoah prayed and asked God to let the angel instruct him too.

When we think about children today and their reactions toward their parents, it seems strange that a mother and a father can actually bring a child up and expect him or her to do what they want them to do. Children want to make their own decisions about who they are and what they are going to do or become in life. They certainly are not trying to hear what their parents are saying about who they are and who their interests and desires should be toward. Imagine telling your child that he/she should surround him/herself with only the things and people that are of God. I know parents that have brought their sons and daughters up in the things of God and expected to see them used mightily in the ministry but have gotten disappointed due to their children taking wrong turns after they reach young adulthood. Some just want to do their own thing and others get hurt in ministry, which is a tragic. Because people who lack true understanding of God's Word, ignorantly mishandles children especially pastors' children, they often become bitter toward the things of God and leave the church.

Apparently, the mother of Samson was a willing vessel who was honored to be used by God. She took care of her body the way that the angel of the LORD told her to, because the boy was a Nazarite. He had strength beyond human belief and was used by God to kill many Philistines which were described as giants. Due to the submissive heart of a woman, God did great exploits through her seed. This was a time that God bruised Satan's or the serpent's head just as he spoke that He would when He spoke to the serpent in the Garden of Eden.

Chapter 7

Ruth and Naomi

There is an entire book in the Bible that tells the story of Naomi and Ruth called the Book of Ruth. This is a beautiful story about a young woman who was introduced to the LORD through marrying a man. After Ruth's husband died, she was left to make a decision of whether to stay with the LORD by staying with her mother-in-law, Naomi or go back to her people and their god. Of course, she firmly decided that her mother-in-law's God was her God and that she would stay with her mother-in-law.

There was a famine in the land of Judah, so Elimelech, Naomi's husband, moved his family to a country, called Moab. They had two sons, Mahlon and Chilion, who married Moabites women, Orpah and Ruth, while they lived there. The family lived in Moab for ten years. During the course of the ten years, Elimelech and his two sons died, and there were no men left in the family to take care of Naomi and her two daughters-in-law. The famine became even greater. In order for Naomi to survive, she decided to go back to the land of Judah because she heard that the LORD was making provision for the people in need there. Naomi and her two daughters-in-law left the place where they were living to go and live in Judah.

When they got to the road that led to the land of Judah before leaving Moab, Naomi kissed her daughters-in-law and told them to go back to their mothers' home. She spoke a prayer over them, **"May the LORD**

show kindness to you as you have shown to your dead and to me. May the LORD grant that each of you will find rest in the home of another husband (Ruth 1:8, NIV)." Naomi cried as she told them good-bye, but they said that they wanted to go with her. Then Naomi told them that she could not give them what they needed in life. She said that she was old and could not have any more sons to give them to marry. Even if that was possible, they would not wait until her sons grew up. They would not remain unmarried. Then Naomi said that the LORD's hand had gone out against her and that they did not have to suffer hardships with her. She assured them that they would be better off with their own mothers in their own country.

After listening to Naomi's reasons for them to stay in Moab, Orpah kissed Naomi good-bye and went back to her mother's house, but Ruth stayed and refused to leave her. Naomi urged Ruth to go back with her sister-in-law. Ruth's reply to her mother-in-law was, **"Don't urge me to leave you or to turn back from you. Where you go I will go, and where you stay I will stay. Your people will be my people and your God my God. Where you die I will die, and there I will be buried. May the LORD deal with me, be it ever so severely, if anything but death separates you and me (Ruth 1:16-17, NIV)."** After Naomi realized that Ruth was serious and determined, she stopped asking her to go back. So, Naomi and Ruth went to Bethlehem in the land of Judah, Naomi's home town. The people in Bethlehem greeted Naomi by her name, but Naomi told them that she left town with a full happy life, but the LORD made her life very bitter due to the fact that she came back empty. Because her husband and sons were no more, all she had was misfortune. So, she told the people not to call her Naomi but called her Mara.

When Naomi and Ruth arrived in Bethlehem the barley harvest was beginning. Ruth asked Naomi could she go out in the field of whomever she found favor with to gather leftover grain behind the harvesters. Naomi gave her permission to go, and she went and picked up grain. Later they found out that she was working in a field that belonged to Boaz, a man that was related to Elimelech, her father-in-law. Boaz saw her working in the field and asked his foreman who she was. The foreman told him that she was the Moabite woman who came back from Moab with Naomi. He told Boaz that Ruth had asked him for permission to gather some leftovers and that she had been working hard since she began to work that day.

So Boaz spoke to Ruth and told her to stay with the servant girls, but do not go and work in the field. He told her to watch the field where the men were harvesting, and the men were told not to touch her. She could get water from the water jars that the men had filled when she became thirsty. Ruth bowed down with her face to the ground and asked him why she had found such favor in his eyes. **"Boaz replied, 'I've been told all about what you have done for your mother-in-law since the death of your husband—how you left your father and mother and your homeland and came to live with a people you did not know before. May the LORD repay you for what you have done. May you be richly rewarded by the LORD, the God of Israel, under whose wings you have come to take refuge (Ruth 2: 11-12, NIV).'"** Ruth said to Boaz that he had comforted her by speaking kindly to her. She asked that she may continue to find favor in his eyes even though she did not have the standing of his servant girls.

At meal time, Boaz invited Ruth to eat bread and vinegar with him. She sat down among the harvesters and ate roasted grain until she was full and had some left over. When she went out to pick up the left over in the field, Boaz told the harvesters to pull out some of their stalks that they gathered and leave them in the field for her. He told them not to embarrass or rebuke her if she gathered among the sheaves. Ruth gathered in the field until evening. After she finished threshing the barley that she had gathered, she had about an ephah. She carried the grain and the leftover food from her meal to her mother-in-law.

Naomi asked her where had she worked that day and she said, **"Blessed be the man who took notice of you (Ruth 2:19, NIV)!"** Ruth told Naomi that the name of the man was Boaz, and she told her about him. Naomi spoke a blessing over Boaz and said that he had not stopped showing kindness to the living and the dead. Then she told Ruth that Boaz was their close relative and who was one of their kinsman-redeemers. Ruth told her mother-in-law that Boaz told her to stay with his servant girls and workers until they finish harvesting all of his grain. Naomi told her that it was good for her to stay with the girls in his field, because she could be harmed in someone else's field. So Ruth stayed with Boaz's servant girls until all the grain, both the wheat and barley was completely harvested.

One day Naomi said to Ruth that she should try to find a home for her where she would be provided for. So she told Ruth to go down to Boaz's threshing floor that night, because he would be winnowing (separating grain from chaff) barley. Naomi told Ruth to take a bath and put on her best clothes and perfume. Then she was to go to the threshing floor but was not to let him know that she was there. After he finished eating, drinking and lay down to sleep, she was to go and uncover his feet and lay down. Naomi told her that Boaz would tell her what to do next. Ruth told Naomi that she would do whatever she asked her to do. So she went down to the threshing floor and did everything that Naomi instructed her to do.

Boaz was startled in the middle of night when he turned over and discovered that a woman was lying at his feet. He asked, **"Who are you (Ruth 3:9, NIV)?"** Ruth answered by saying that she was his servant Ruth. Then she asked him to spread the corner of his garment over her, since he was a kinsman-redeemer. Boaz replied, **"The LORD bless you, my daughter. This kindness is greater than that you showed earlier: You have not run after the younger men, whether rich or poor. And now, my daughter, don't be afraid. I will do for you all you ask. All my fellow townsmen know that you are a woman of noble character. Although it is true that I am near of kin, there is a kinsman-redeemer nearer than I. Stay here for the night, and in the morning if he wants to redeem, good; let him redeem. But if he is not willing, as surely as the LORD lives I will do it. Lie here until morning (Ruth 3: 10-14, NIV)."**

Ruth laid at Boaz feet until the morning but got up early so no one would know that she had spent the night with Boaz. Before she left he gave her six measures of barley to take home for Naomi and her. After Ruth told her mother-in-law about her night with Boaz, Naomi told her to wait for the man would not rest until the matter was settled that day.

That morning Boaz went to the town gate and waited until the kinsman-redeemer whom he had mentioned to Ruth came along. Boaz asked him to come and sit with him along with ten elders of the town. Then he told the man that Naomi had come back from Moab and was selling the piece of land that belonged to their brother Elimelech. Boaz suggested to the man to buy the land, because he was the first in line to buy the property. The man said that he would buy it. Then Boaz told him that the day when he buys the land, he would also be getting Elimelech's widow, in order to maintain the name of the dead with his property. After hearing he would be acquiring a widow, the kinsman-redeemer declined to buy the property. He told Boaz that he could redeem it for himself, because that might put his estate in danger. So the two men made an agreement in front of the ten elders as witnesses that Boaz could redeem the land. Boaz also announced to the elders and the kinsman-redeemer that he had bought the property of Elimelech, Kilion and Mahlon from Naomi and that he had acquired Ruth the Moabitess, Mahlon's widow as his wife to keep the dead man's name from disappearing from the town records. Then the elders acknowledged the legal proceedings and spoke the kinds of blessings upon Boaz and his marriage to Ruth that compared to the blessings spoken upon Rachel, Leah and Tamar who were mothers in the line of Judah.

Then Boaz made Ruth his wife, and when they consummated their marriage, the LORD caused her to conceive. She gave birth to a son whom they named Obed. The women were very happy for Naomi, because they said to her **"Praise be to the LORD, who this day has not left you without a kinsman-redeemer. May he become famous throughout Israel! He will renew your life and sustain you in your old age. For your daughter-in-law, who loves you and who is better to you than seven sons, has given him birth (Ruth 4: 14-15, NIV)."** Then Naomi cared for the child as her own, and the women in the town said that the child was Naomi's child. Obed was the father of Jesse, and Jesse was the father of David. They belonged to the family or the tribe of Judah, whose son was Perez and down the family line came Hezron, Ram, Amminadab, Nahshon, Salmon, and Boaz.

We see God using Ruth to keep Judah's descendants living on throughout generations. Keep in mind that Judah's son was Perez whose mother was Tamar. So Ruth, the Moabitess has a son that is in the direct line of Judah. Because Ruth chose her mother-in-law's God, God showed her favor and saw to it that she got another husband who was able to take care of her for the rest of her life. Not only did she get a husband, she also had a son, who represented more fulfillments. Ruth got a taste of Naomi's God and His goodness; therefore, she refused to turn around and go back to a people and their gods that could not give her happiness or eternal life. The revelation of God that she had obtained from being with her dead husband's family was for sure, and she declared it when she told her mother-in-law that her people were the same as her people and that her God will be hers also. Ruth caught a hold to her eternal destination, and she was not about to let it go.

Ruth depicts faithfulness, dedication, loyalty and true love. Her name means companion, friend, and vision of beauty. Notice the scripture says that when the women were talking to Naomi, they told her that her daughter-in-law was better to her than seven sons. Sons are not often as dedicated to their mothers as daughters are. Ruth stood by her mother-in-law, and she worked to provide for her. By clinging to Naomi, we can see that she held her mother-in-law in very high esteem. Ruth's love for her mother-in-law and her obedience to her caused her to end up with a happy, fulfilled life. She became a widow at an early age which forced her to have to make a decision about what she would do for the rest of her life. Naomi urged her to go back to her mother's house and to stay among her people so that she may find another husband and be provided for. But Ruth saw no good future with her people. She had gotten a glimpse of life with a true living God and a people that God favored. The Bible does not record any words of complaint from her. She just acted as an obedient daughter to her mother-in-law. By doing so, she and Naomi were able to enjoy life again with someone providing for them.

Naomi depicts broken-heartedness, hurt and confusion about her life and God. She told her daughters-in-law that it was more bitter (harsh) for her than for them, because the hand of the LORD had gone out against her. Naomi expressed her feelings further when she and Ruth arrived in Bethlehem. When the women greeted her and called her by name, she said, **"Don't call me Naomi. Call me Mara, because the almighty has made my life very bitter, I went away full, but the LORD brought me back empty. Why call me Naomi? The LORD has afflicted me; the almighty has brought misfortune upon me (Ruth 1:20-21, NIV)."** The name Naomi means pleasant, graceful or delightful, but these meanings did not describe her at that point in time. Naomi felt that God was punishing her by taking away her husband and two sons. As we read her words, we can hear the brokenness and the grief that she was feeling. We can also see a grieving heart of a wife who was now a widow and a loving mother who had lost all of her children. We can see a woman who felt that she once had a family, and all were going well. Although she moved away with her husband and sons because of famine or lack, she felt secure because they had each other to love and help each other. But when they all died, she felt that she had been left alone in the world to care for herself with no one to help her.

Naomi probably had no idea of where or how to start providing for herself which is another reason that may have explained why she told her daughters-in-law to go back to their mothers' homes. She could not provide for herself more or less two daughters-in-law. But God changed things around for her by giving her wisdom to direct her daughter-in-law, Ruth in the right direction. First of all, God did not leave her all along, because Ruth never left her. Ruth staying with Naomi reminds us of God who never leave nor forsake us. Through Ruth's faithfulness and loyalty toward Naomi, God caused Naomi to have a full and happy life again. Instead of feeling afflicted and misfortune, Boaz, Ruth and Obed made her feel that she was loved, needed, rejuvenated and fortunate. Naomi probably thanked God daily for restoring life back into her.

On the other hand, Naomi's thoughts were not completely consumed with her hurts and misfortunes. She thought about Ruth's well-being as well. Naomi could not help being appreciative toward Ruth, because Ruth took it upon herself to go gather their food daily. Naomi had to be sure that Ruth would be provided for and cared for the rest of her life like any mother would. Because of her concern and love for Ruth, she instructed Ruth in details of how to conduct herself one night with Boaz. Naomi also led Ruth to Boaz, because she knew the sincerity and kindness of his heart. After Ruth followed Naomi's instructions to the letter, the rest of the story became history.

The story of Ruth and Naomi paints a beautiful picture of love, humility and servant hood. The two women illustrate what can happen when two people agree and work together toward the same goal. They lived in harmony and were concerned about one another to the point that they took care of each other without ever thinking of leaving each other. Therefore, when God blessed one, the other one got blessed also, and good things happened for both of them in the same blessings. *OH WHAT AN AWESOME, WONDERFUL GOD!* Their story shows us that God will see to it that our needs are met even if we are women left alone to care for ourselves. We don't always see our way, but God always make the way for us. Ruth and Naomi exhibited all of the attributes of love toward each other, and in the end their sorrow turned into joy. I am sure that they never forgot about Naomi's husband and sons. No, they could never be replaced, but God gave them other people to love and care for. In the end it became very clear to them that God cared for them, because they are named in the direct line of David and Jesus as their fore mothers.

Chapter 8

HANNAH

Hannah was married to Elkanah who had another wife besides her, named Peninnah. Peninnah had sons and daughters, but Hannah had no children. Peninnah used the fact that she had given their husband children to taunt and provoke Hannah. It grieved Hannah very much that she had no children and that Peninnah provoked her with the fact. Once every year Elkanah took his family to Shiloh to worship and to make sacrifice to the LORD. When making sacrifice, he would give Peninnah and their children portions of the meat. But he gave a double portion of meat to Hannah, because he loved her. Elkanah saw her hurts and heavy grief. Hannah would cry and not eat due to Peninnah taunting her and because she wanted children. Her husband tried to comfort and console her by asking her why was she crying and not eating? He would ask her didn't he mean more to her than ten sons?

One time when Elkanah took his family to Shiloh to worship and make sacrifice to the LORD, Hannah went into the temple after her family had finished eating and drinking. Hannah was bitter in her soul; therefore, she desperately cried out to the LORD. While she was praying, she made a vow to the LORD saying, **"O LORD Almighty, if you will only look upon your servant's misery and remember me, and not forget your servant but give her a son, then I will give him to the LORD for all the days of his life, and no razor will ever be used on his head (I Samuel 1:11, NIV)."**

When she entered the temple Eli, the priest was sitting by the doorpost in a chair. As she prayed, he watched her lips and saw them moving. But he could not hear what she was saying, because she was praying in her heart and in a soft voice. So, Eli thought that she was drunk, and he told her to get rid of the drinking and her wine. Hannah responded by saying, **"Not so, my lord. I am a woman who is deeply troubled. I have not been drinking wine or beer; I was pouring out my soul to the LORD. Do not take your servant for a wicked woman; I have been praying here out of my great anguish and grief (I Samuel 1: 15-16, NIV)."** Eli told her to go in peace, and may the God of Israel grant her what she had asked Him for. Hannah salutation to Eli was that she may find favor in his eyes. Then she left and ate something, and her face was no longer downcast.

The next morning Elkanah and his family arose early and worshiped the LORD. Then they went back to Ramah where their home was. Elkanah and Hannah engaged in intercourse and the LORD caused her to conceive. She had a baby boy who she named Samuel. Hannah gave him that name because she said, **"I asked the LORD for him (I Samuel 1: 20, NIV)."**

Later sometime after Samuel's birth, the time came for Elkanah to go for their annual offering of sacrifices to the LORD. But Hannah told her husband that she would stay at home and wait until Samuel was weaned then she would take him and present him before the LORD. She said that he will live there in the temple always. Elkanah told her to stay and do whatever she thought was best. Hannah stayed at home and cared for Samuel until he was weaned. Then she took him, a three-year old bull, an ephah of flour and a skin of wine to the house of the LORD in Shiloh. After they sacrificed the bull, they took the child (toddler) to Eli the priest. Then Hannah said to him, **"As surely as you live, my lord, I am the woman who stood here beside you praying to the LORD. I prayed for this child, and the LORD has granted me what I asked of him. So now I give him to the Lord. For his whole life he will be given over to the LORD (I Samuel 1: 26-28, NIV)."**

Hannah prayed and boasted about what the LORD had done for her in I Samuel 2. She spoke of how God had brought joy to her heart and how He had silenced her enemies. Hannah proclaimed that she was barren, but God gave her several children. She told about how The LORD can bring life to something that is dead; how He humbles those who boast and operate in pride; how He lifts the poor from the dust and puts them on thrones in high places and how he exalts the humble. Hannah boasted about the LORD awesomeness. She made known that it is not wise to oppose the LORD, because He will shatter all that are oppositional and defiance toward him.

Hannah made Samuel a little robe every year and took it to him when she and her husband went to offer their annual sacrifice to the LORD. Eli would bless Elkanah and Hannah by saying to Elkanah, **"May the LORD give you children by this woman to take the place of the one she prayed for and gave to the LORD (I Samuel 2:20, NIV)."** Hannah had three sons and two daughters later, because the LORD was gracious to her. But Samuel grew up in the temple in the presence of the LORD ministering unto the LORD daily.

Hannah got God's attention by pouring her heart out to Him in her time of pain and despair. Undoubtedly, she was suffering with deep emotional and heart aching pains which had thrown her into deep depression. We know this because she showed all the symptoms and signs of major depression. Hannah cried constantly; she had no appetite and would not eat; therefore, her energy was probably almost gone. She felt incomplete and useless due to the inability to have children. After all, becoming a mother is what most women feel is one of their main purposes for being on this earth. Like most women, Hannah wanted to feel complete through the experience of being a mother, because mothers are what the vast majority of women are. I am sure that she had many negative thoughts. Hannah probably felt inadequate, worthless and thought that she was not capable of having children. These thoughts usually accompany unfulfilled desires, and she was unfulfilled.

Not only did Hannah battle with feelings of worthlessness, she also had to deal with feelings that caused her to wonder just how her husband really felt about her since she could not give him children. Satan probably had a good time flooding her mind with thoughts that told her she was not pleasing to her husband. Although he tried to comfort her with words and acts of giving her more meat than her rival, these things would not bring fulfillment and comfort to her. She probably thought that he was just saying things and acting a certain way toward her to make her feel better.

Besides, her husband had another wife who had given him children that lived in close proximity with her, Peninnah. Every day Hannah had to live with a rival who seemed to have had everything that she wanted. To make matters even worse for Hannah, Peninnah picked, poked and antagonized her due to the fact that she had given their husband children and Hannah had not. Like Hannah, Peninnah probably thought that Hannah could not have children. She also saw their husband treating Hannah better than he treated her. But Peninnah had an edge on Hannah. So, she decided that she would use what she had to make Hannah's life miserable. Peninnah said to Hannah in her antagonizing way that Elkanah may give her more than he gives her (Peninnah), but she has to know that he cares about her (Peninnah) too, because she was the one who had given him offsprings. So, she constantly rubbed that information in Hannah's face. This situational relationship reminds us of Leah and Rachel. There were trouble and turmoil going on within their household, because God said the two shall be one, not the three. No woman should have to share her husband with another woman just like no man should share his wife with another man.

One day Hannah had an epiphany. She decided to call on the only one who could deliver her out of her misery. Hannah found her way to the temple where God dwelt, and she got on her face before him and cried out to him in desperation and agony. She was in need of help, and she knew that no one could help her but God. In her desperate state of mind, she asked God to bless her with a child, a son to be exact. As she cried and prayed, she asked Him to look upon her misery and deliver her. While praying and asking for a son, Hannah made God a promise that if He would give her a son, she would give him back to Him. Her son would serve Him all of his life and would be raised up under His priest caring for the house of the LORD and ministering to Him.

Hannah spoke a word that was released in the atmosphere over her soon to be son. She vowed or promised God that she would give him back to Him and that he would serve Him for all of his days or for his entire life. *OH Boy! What a word!* Imagine a mother wanting a child, a son so bad that she would pledge to give him up if she could just have him. That was exactly what she did. Hannah was true to her promised. After God granted her request or plea, she took her son to the temple of the LORD and left him with the high priest to grow up in the presence of the LORD. It had to have been difficult for her to give her very young child to someone else to rear. Samuel was probably around two year old, since he had just been weaned from her breast. He was her only child, and the seed that she so desired to give her husband. Also, it was amazing that her husband agreed to let her give him to the priest to be his primary caretaker or in essence his foster parent, his father. But, it was clear that Elkanah and Hannah both loved the LORD; therefore, they knew that placing their child in God's care was the best thing that they could ever do.

Nevertheless, Hannah knew what she had promised the LORD, and she knew that she could not go back on her promise to Him. Hannah's attitude was so unselfish. She could have tried to raise her son in her own house and teach him everything that she could about the LORD. That's what most people would do. But because of the wisdom and a true heart of worship that I believed that Hannah had, she took her young child to the house of the LORD. Hannah knew that the LORD dwelt there, and she wanted her son to be where the LORD was. There was no better place to learn all the things of the LORD or how to serve Him than being in the house of the LORD. By making this decision and committing Samuel into the hands of the LORD, she shielded him from having to grow up around his brothers and sisters whose mother did not like her. Samuel did not have to go through the ridicule from Elkanah's second family or to see the turmoil that his mother was experiencing. He did not have to be subjected to what Isaac went through with Hagar and Ishmael or what Joseph went through with his brothers, who mothers were different from his. Samuel was reared in the presence of the LORD, and he learned first-hand what would please the LORD. What a wonderful way to be brought up. The child and man Samuel could not help but to be special to God.

Hannah spoke Samuel's purpose, calling and destiny on him before he was even conceived in her womb. In the past, God had sent an angel to speak to a woman and man to tell them about the child that they would conceive and bring up. God would tell them through his angel what was the child's purpose in the earth, but this time it was different. Hannah told God what her first born son would do in relation to Him. Since she spoke it, she was determined to do everything in her power to see to it that her promise to God would come into flourishing even if it hurt her to give him up. After leaving him in the care of the priest, Hannah knew what she had done and what she promised God that she would do. Because of Hannah's brave act, the Scriptures say that Samuel served the LORD all the days of his life. Not only is Samuel known for serving and ministering to the LORD from a very young child, but every word that he prophesied as a prophet came to pass. The Bible says that God caused none of his words to fall to the ground (I Samuel 3:9). God called Samuel into the priesthood and anointed him as His priest and prophet. Samuel was the voice of God to the Israelite people after the priest, Eli died. Samuel became an awesome powerful man of God. God used him, because he loved and served God with all of his heart, soul and his body daily. He served in complete obedience to the LORD, because he followed his commands without hesitations. His mother must have been awfully proud of him.

Now Hannah did not have to be sad and broken-hearted. She walked in healing and victory, because God did not leave Hannah wishing that she should have reared Samuel. He caused her to give birth to three more sons and two daughters to rear up in her own household. God filled her house with children who she could hold, caress, and love on. But she did not ever forget that Samuel was her child. Hannah made him a robe every year and took it to him while visiting and he knew who his biological parents were. God gave her other children for her fulfillment and also to shut her rival's mouth. I can see Hannah now saying to Peninnah, look what God did for me! With that said, Peninnah could do or say nothing but be ashamed of her foolishness. Hannah's story is another testimony of God turning Hannah's misery into her miracles, one after another. Her mourning was over, and she had joy unspeakable. Hannah envisioned and spoke a prophet into existence without knowing that she was doing so, and God blessed her beyond her wildest dream. Hannah left her mark in the earth, and her name will always be remembered. Because of her pain, she gave birth to one of the most powerful and accurate prophets that has ever lived on earth.

Chapter 9

Esther

There was a time in history that Xerxes reigned as King in Babylon over 127 provinces. He displayed vast wealth of his kingdom, his splendor and his glory for 180 days. When the 180 day celebration ended, he gave a great banquet that lasted seven days in his palace's garden. The garden was beautifully adorned with expensive materials, such as silver and gold furniture and pure gold goblets for drinking wine. After drinking a lot of wine, the king got excited and commanded that his wife, Queen Vashti be brought before him wearing her royal crown. He wanted to display her beauty to his nobles and the people, because she was lovely to look at. Queen Vashti refused to come; therefore, King Xerxes became furious and extremely angry. Since it was customary for the king to seek advice from wise men who had been selected by him for counsel, he asked the wise men what he should do about the queen's refusal. The wise men advised him to never let the queen come into his presence again and to replace her with another queen. Of course they made their decision in order to keep their wives in subjection to them. The king did as they advised him to do.

One day, the king remembered his wife and what he had decreed about her which left him with no wife. Then King Xerxes' personal attendants suggested that he would order a search for beautiful virgins to be brought to the palace for the king to choose a wife from. The king took their advice, and a search went out throughout the provinces. Young virgins were brought to live in a certain part of the palace to be groomed and beautified for a period of time. The virgins had to go through a process of treatments and beautifications for a whole year before they were ready to appear before the king.

Esther was one of the beautiful young virgins that had been chosen to appear before the king. She was a Jew from the tribe of Benjamin at that time in Babylon, because her people had been captured and taken into exile by Nebuchadnezzar when he was king. Apparently, her mother and father died when she was very young, because she was adopted and reared by her cousin Mordecai as his own daughter. Esther's real name or her Jewish's birth name was Hadassah. During that time all of the Israelites who had been taken captives were given Babylonians' names and taught Babylonians' customs. In order words, they were reprogrammed or transformed into Babylonians, (so the Babylonians thought). This was Nebuchadnezzar's brilliant way of keeping the whole world in subjection under his reign, because the entire world was under one ruler. Esther was taken to the citadel of Susa and placed under the care of Hegai who was in charge of the harem, which was a section of the palace reserved for women. Esther had a lovely body form and beautiful facial features. She won Hegai's favor from the moment he saw her. Hegai began to give her beauty treatments and special foods right away. He also moved her into the best place in the harem after assigning her seven maids that he selected from the king's palace.

Mordecai forbidded Esther to tell anyone that she was Jewish or anything about her nationality or family background; so she kept her true identity a secret. He kept a check on her by walking back and forth near the courtyard of the harem to find out how she was and what was happening to her. The time came for Esther to appear before the king. She could have had anything that she desired to go before the king, but she only asked for the things that Hegai suggested. Esther won the favor of everyone who saw her. When she appeared before the king, she won his favor too. The king chose her over all of the other virgin girls. He set a crown on her head and had a banquet in honor of her; the king gave the banquet for his nobles and officials. He gave away gifts freely and declared the banquet day a holiday. Esther became his queen; therefore, replacing Vashti.

Esther continued to follow Mordecai's instructions but kept her identity a secret just as he told her to do. One day Mordecai overheard two of the king's officials, Bigthana and Teresh, plotting to kill the king. Mordecai told Esther, and she reported it to the king giving Mordecai the credit for telling her. After the king had them investigated, he determined that they were in deed planning to kill him, he immediately had them hanged.

Afterward, King Xerxes gave Haman a seat of honoi. He placed him over all of the other nobles; therefore, all of the officials had to kneel down and pay honor to him according to the king's command. Mordecai did not bow down nor give him honor. Some of the officials asked Mordecai why he was disobeying the King's order. Mordecai told them that he was a Jew, and it was not their custom to bow down to a man. As a matter of fact, it was forbidden by the LORD for them to bow down to a man. Because Mordecai would not obey the king's command after a period of the officials appealing to him, they told Haman. When Haman saw for himself that Mordecai would not kneel down or pay him honor, he became very enraged and sought a way to destroy not only Mordecai but all of the Jews: men, women, children and babies. Haman told the king that Mordecai and the Jewish people did not obey his commands and that the whole race of Jewish people was a threat to his kingdom and to his rulership. So, the king issued an edict or a decree in citadel of Susa to totally destroy and annihilate all of the Jews, young and old.

When Mordecai heard the news, he tore his clothes, put on sackcloth and ashes, and began to cry loudly and bitterly in the open city at the king's gate. The Jewish people were mourning, fasting, weeping and wailing in every city that the decree had gone to. Esther's maids and eunuchs told her that Mordecai was at the king's gate in sackcloth and ashes mourning. She sent him some clothes to put on, but he refused them. Then she ordered Hathach, one of the eunuchs that were assigned to her, to find out what was troubling Mordecai. Hathach went to Mordecai, and Mordecai told him everything that Haman had done for the demised of the Jews. He told him that Haman had even pledged to put a certain amount of money into the royal treasure for the destruction of the Jews. Mordecai sent a copy of the published text that the king issued for the destruction of the Jews to Esther and told Hathach to urge her to go before the king to beg for mercy and plead with him for her people. Esther sent word back to him that she could not just appear before the king, because it was the king's law that whoever appeared before him without being summoned first would be put to death. The only exception was that the king extends his gold scepter to her and invites her in to see him. She added that thirty days had gone by since she was summoned to be in the king's presence.

When Mordecai heard her reply, he told the eunuch to tell her that just because she was in the king's house that she was not to think for one moment that her life would be saved. He also said that she and her family would perish, but God would send someone else to deliver the Jews. Mordecai stated that she may have been placed into her royal position for the purpose of delivering her people. No one could be for sure, but this task could be her divine opportunity to do something great for God and her people.

Then Esther sent Mordecai a reply requesting that he would go throughout Susa and gather all the Jews and ask them to fast with her for three days and three nights without food or drink. She said that her maids would fast too, and when the days and nights of fasting were done, she would go to the king. Esther stated, **"even though it is against the law. And if I perish, I perish (Esther 4:16, NIV)."** Mordecai carried out Queen Esther's instructions.

After the days of fasting was finished, Esther put on her royal robe and went into the inner court of the palace. She stood in front of the king's hall. The king saw her because he was sitting on his royal throne facing the entrance of the hall, and he was pleased with her. So he extended his gold scepter out to her that she may touch the tip of it. Esther accepted the invitation. The king asked her, What was her request? He told her that he would give her as much as half of the kingdom if she wanted it.

But Esther prayerfully and wisely planned the right moment as to when and how she would appeal to the king for mercy for her and her people. She asked the king and Haman, the man who had planned her demise, to attend a banquet which she would sponsor. Esther knew that the king loved to wine and dine. So, she wanted him in a good, happy mood when she made her request. She also knew that Haman would be delighted to come, because he would have felt that he was being honored above everyone else by the king and queen. As a matter of fact, that was exactly what he told his wife and friends. Esther prepared a banquet for them for two consecutive days.

After the first banquet, Haman left very happy and conceited, but he noticed that Mordecai continued not to pay him honor after he walked by him; this made him very angry. Nevertheless, he went home and bragged to his wife and friends about his wealth and being the only one invited as an honored guest to the queen's two banquets. Then he told them about when he was leaving the palace and saw Mordecai. Mordecai did not fear him, and he became angry. So, his wife and friends suggested that he build a gallows seventy-five feet high and ask the king to have Mordecai hanged the next morning on it. They told him to then go and enjoy himself with the king and queen at the banquet that the queen had invited him to. Haman loved the idea and had the gallows built.

Because the LORD intervened, the king could not sleep that night. He ordered his servant to bring the book of chronicles, which was a record of his reign to him. He read that Mordecai was the one who reported that two of the king's officers were conspiring to kill the king. The king asked what had been done to honor Mordecai. The servants answered nothing that they knew of.

Early that morning Haman entered the outer court of the palace to ask the king about hanging Mordecai. The king attendants or servants told him that Haman was there in the outer court. The king ordered them to bring him in. After Haman came in, **the king asked him, What should be done for the man the king delights to honor (Esther 6: 6, NIV)?**" This pleased Haman, because he was sure the king was talking about him. He told the king to have his servants bring one of his royal robes that he had worn and a horse that he had ridden with a royal crest placed on its head. Then have the servants to put the robe on the man that the king would delight to honor and lead him on the horse through the city main streets. While the man is riding on the horse, have someone to proclaim that, that was the man the king delighted to honor. The king commanded Haman to get the robe and the horse and then honor Mordecai the way in which he suggested. He told him to be sure not to leave any of the details out. Haman grudgingly followed the king orders.

After Mordecai was honored, he went back to his place of grief. Haman went home afterwards in shame and grief. He told his advisors and his wife what had happened. The wise men and his wife told him that he could not stand against Mordecai and that he would be ruined, because Mordecai was of the Jewish seed and would be the start of his downfall. Then one of the king's eunuchs came in and escorted Haman to the second banquet that Esther had prepared.

So the king and Haman went to Esther's banquet of wine, and the king asked her again what her request was. Again he told her that he would give her up to half of the kingdom if she asked for it. Esther answered by saying, **"If I have found favor with you, O king, and if it pleases your majesty, grant me my life—this is my petition. And spare my people—this is my request. For I and my people have been sold for destruction and slaughter and annihilation. If we had merely been sold as male and female slaves, I would have kept quiet, because no such distress would justify disturbing the king"** **(Esther 7:3-4, NIV).** The king asked who this man was and where was he that would dare do such a thing. Esther replied, **"The adversary and enemy is this vile Haman"** **(Esther 7:6, NIV).**

The king became very angry and enraged. He went outside into the palace garden. Haman became terrified, because he knew that the king had already decided that he would die from the look on his face. So he did not go after the king, instead he stayed behind to beg Esther for his life. About the same time the king was coming back in Haman was falling on the couch where Esther was sitting in a reclining position.

The king perceived that Haman was trying to molest his wife while they were in the house with him.

The king's guards immediately covered Haman's face after the king spoke his perception. Then one of the king's eunuchs told the king that Haman had built a gallows seventy-five feet high at his house specifically for Mordecai, the man who had helped the king. The king told them to hang Haman on the gallows that he had built. Then the king's anger was appeased.

Esther told the king that Mordecai was related to her and how he was related to her. The king gave Esther Haman's estate, and Esther in turn appointed Mordecai over the estate. The king gave Mordecai his signet ring that he had reclaimed back from Haman before he was hanged.

Again Esther begged the king to revoke the order that Haman had sent out to kill and destroy the Jews. She fell at his feet and cried for mercy. When the king extended his gold scepter to her, she rose up before him and said that if he regards her with favor and if he is pleased with her, then overrule the dispatches that Haman had devised and wrote to destroy her and her people.

The king told Esther and Mordecai that no document written in the king's name and sealed with his signet ring could be revoked. But he added that they could write another decree since he had given them Haman's estate and the king's signet ring. The king went on further and told them to write the decree in the name of the king or his name and seal it with his signet ring. So, a decree went out that said the Jews could and should take up arms and defend themselves against anyone who would attack them. The Jews mourning then turned into joy. When the day came for them to be attacked, the Jews were ready to fight. They defeated their enemies by killing thousands of them. Some of the native people became Jews, because they feared Mordecai. Mordecai became second in rank to the king, and the Jewish people made the days that they defeated their enemies, days of remembrance with celebrating and feasting.

In the midst of defeating their enemies, the Jews killed Haman's ten sons. Queen Esther asked the king to have them hanged on the gallows, and the king granted her request. Mordecai wore royal garments and was remembered and respected as the man who spoke up for his people.

God placed Esther in position and saw to it that she found favor with the king and with Haman; although Haman had planned her destruction but did not know. This shows that Satan does not always see what is coming, nor does he know who God has in place to bring him down when he gets too high and too mighty. Haman thought he had everything a man could desire, and he probably did. But he decided to make God his enemy by making God's chosen people his enemy. He despised Mordecai and the Jews, because they would not bow down and pay honor to him. How many times do we see men and women develop hatred in their hearts for people who do not think that they are so wonderful? Just as Haman did, they began by talking about the people who do not honor or praise them. They easily forget that all the honor and praise belong to God alone. So, they go about sowing seeds of discord in other hearts about the people who they perceive that do not honor or like them. Because of the strife that they carry, best of friends have separated, siblings have parted and marriages have been destroyed. In some cases, murder or physical death has even occurred all because man thinks too highly of himself (Romans 12:3).

Haman did not know that his orders to annihilate all the Jewish people included the Queen. But even if he did know, he probably would have been happy to see her die too. After all, the wise men had already advised the king to get rid of his first queen, Vashti. That advice was given strictly to benefit them not the king and his wife. They wanted to put fear in their own wives to keep them subjective to them. They never thought twice about the cruelty that they inflicted on the queen or the king. They did not care that the king or the queen's hearts would be broken, or that they had to go through a period of being without a spouse. They had their spouses, and were undoubtedly satisfied in their marriages. The wise men clearly were used by the devil to come between the king and his wife.

But this time when the order was given to get rid of the Queen, God intervened. In spite of her fears, Esther allowed God to use her; therefore, all of the Jewish people's lives were saved from destruction and annihilation. Not only did she keep the Jews from being destroyed, she also had no pity on Haman and his household. Esther requested that Haman and all ten of his sons be hanged on the gallows that he built for Mordecai and the Jews. This reminds us of the saying, 'if you dig a ditch for someone else, you will fall in it.' Now, Queen Esther is noticed as one of the great women of God who was put in place at the right time to deal with the enemy of God. God truly takes care of his own.

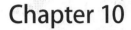

Chapter 10

Other Old Testament Women Used by God

There are other women in the Old Testament that God used who made tremendous impacts in history such as: Michal, Abigail and Bathsheba. Also, God used the women who simply obeyed the Prophet Elijah and the Prophet Elisha. God used them during strategic moments. They were used to take care of some of the mighty and anointed men of God. Some acted while risking their lives, but God saw to it that they came out victorious.

Michal

You can find the story of Michal, who was King Saul's daughter, and David's first wife in the Book of I Samuel 19: 11-17. King Saul gave Michal to David as a part of the payment or reward for David killing Goliath, the giant that terrorized the Jewish army. You have heard the story of how David killed Goliath with a slingshot and a smooth stone. After David killed the giant, he fought as a soldier in the army against the Philistines. The women began to praise David for his heroism, but King Saul became jealous of David and wanted him dead. As part of his first proclamation of reward to the man that killed Goliath, he promised to give his oldest daughter in marriage, but gave her to another man instead. Then because of his burning desire to see David destroyed, he added another battle, one that he thought David would surely be killed fighting. He sent word to David to bring him a hundred Philistines foreskins in order for him to marry his second daughter, Michal. David and his men went in and took two hundred Philistines' foreskins. Then David brought them to Saul. Then Saul saw that God was surely with David. He gave his daughter Michal to David as his wife. The Bible points out that Michal loved David anyway, and David probably felt the same for her. When Saul saw his daughter's love for David and God's favor upon him, he became afraid of him and remained his enemy for the rest of his life.

But because of his jealousy, King Saul became driven to rid his kingdom and himself of David. He could not stand it that David was praised and thought of as a mightier man than he was. So, he made several attempts to kill David. Saul threw a spear at David while he was playing his harp for him, but David quickly got out of the path of the spear. The spear stuck into the wall. Saul had already told his son Jonathan and some of his men to kill David, but they did not. So, he ordered some of the men to watch his house and to kill him in the early morning. Michal warned David and told him that if he did not escape in the night, he would surely be dead by the morning. So, she helped him get away by letting him down through a high window, and he ran. Then Michal put an idol in David's bed, covered it up with clothing, and placed goat's hair at the head. Saul sent men to capture David, but Michal told them that he was sick in bed. After reporting back to Saul, he sent them back and told them to bring him David even if they had to bring the bed with him in it, so he could kill him. The men went back to get David and found the idol. Then Saul asked Michal why she deceived him and helped his enemy get away. Michal told her father that David threatened to kill her if she did not help him.

Michal knew her father well enough to know that she had to tell him a lie about David's escape. Because if she had told him the truth or if he thought that she had helped David escaped, then Saul, her father probably would have had her killed as well. So, Michal, who was a woman that loved her husband, risked her life to help save him from being killed by the king, her father. After her heroic act, she had no idea of what her fate would be, but God saw to it that the king did not kill her. However, the king did give her to another man to be his wife. But in the end, during the last years of her life, she was reunited with her husband, David.

Abigail

Next we see God using another one of David's wife in I Samuel, Chapter 25. This is the story of how David and Abigail met and were married. Abigail was the wife of Nabal, a wealthy man. The Bible described Nabal as being surly and mean in his dealings. One of his servants described him as being a wicked man whom no one could talk to. As David and his men were moving from place to place to avoid the wrath of Saul against them, they set up camp in Carmel near Nabal's property for a while. David and his men were approximately six hundred in number by that time, and they were hungry. David sent some of his men to ask Nabal to provide food for them. This was during the time the harvest was ripe and being put up for storage. David told his men to greet Nabal warmly and to tell him how they had protected him and how they had been kind to him while they camped near him in Carmel. When the men talked to Nabal, he answered harshly and said to them who is Jesse's son that he should give him anything.

The men reported back to David Nabal's response. Then David told four hundred of his men to arm themselves, and he armed himself also. He swore that he would not leave any of the males of Nabal's house alive. They armed themselves and started toward Nabal's house.

In the meantime, as soon as David's men left Nabal's presence, one of Nabal's servants told his wife, Abigail how Nabal had responded to the men David sent to ask for food or provision. Abigail wasted no time. She began immediately to gather food for David and his army.

After she had their servants to load several donkeys with plenty of food, she got on a donkey herself and went to David. Before David and his army reached Nabal's house, Abigail met them. She got off of her donkey and bowed down before David and his army. Then she gave him the provision that she had brought for them while begging for forgiveness on her husband's behalf. She also prophesied to David that he was being sought after by Saul for no other reason than to be killed, because he was certain to become the king. David accepted the provision and told her that he was on his way to kill every male in Nabal's house. He also accepted her apology. Then David and his men turned around and went back to their camps with the donkeys loaded with the food that Abigail gave them.

When Abigail returned home, Nabal was having a great banquet; whereas he was set up and acting as a king. She waited until the next morning to tell him about her meeting with David. After telling him, he had a heart attack and died ten days later. Although David had decided to let him live, God did not. Nabal's heart was evil; therefore it failed him. When David heard about his death, he sent Abigail a message asking her to become his wife and she did.

The Bible describes Abigail as an intelligent and beautiful woman. She was smart and full of wisdom. Because of her wisdom, she saved all the males of Nabal's house. Although it was against her husband's will at that time, she did not think twice about what Nabal wanted. She did the right thing. The Bible does not tell or even give a hint of what Nabal would have done to her for giving David provision without his permission, but I can imagine that her consequences probably would not have been pleasant. After all, she took the authority and went over his head to do the right thing. Afterward Nabal was not allowed to deal with her in any kind of way, because his health failed him. One could explore the reasons for his heart failure. His heart attacked could have been caused because of his fear that David was about to take his life; maybe it was his anger against what his wife did coupled with anger that a large amount of his possessions have been given to David; or perhaps it was a combination of both. Whatever the case was, he was not allowed to live any longer, and Abigail was free of him. So, Abigail is remembered for her act of righteousness toward God's man despite her husband's wishes which saved the lives of all the males in her household including the servants.

Bathsheba

Bathsheba had to take the lead in saving her son Solomon's life as well as her own in I Kings 1. After David became very old and bed ridden, his son Adonijah convinced one of the priest and one of David's close official to agree that he should be king after David. Adonijah was described as being very handsome and assertive. In other words, he got his way most of the time. David apparently did not enforce rules on him, because the Bible says that David did not ask him why he acted the way he did. So, he had a great, big celebration proclaiming that he was to be the next king after his father David, and he had the endorsements of the Priest Abiathar and Joab, who was one of David's close top officials. Adonijah invited all of his brothers who were David's sons except Solomon and his mother, Bathsheba. Also, he did not invite Nathan the Prophet or Zadok the Priest, because they were not in agreement with him.

Nathan the Prophet went to Bathsheba and asked her did she know that Adonijah was putting himself forward as the king without David knowing it. He advised her that in order to save her son's life and her own life, she had to go to David and remind him that he had promised her that Solomon would be king after him. He further told her that while she was talking to David he would appear before the king to say the same thing. Bathsheba followed the advice to the letter, and Nathan came in to see the king while Bathsheba was still talking to him just as he said he would. David told them that Solomon were to be the king after him just as he had sworn to them. Then David called in Zadok the priest, Nathan the prophet and Benaiah son of Jehoiada and told them to take Solomon his son, set him on his own mule and take him to Gihon. In Gihon, Nathan and Zadok were to anoint Solomon as king over Israel, blow the trumpet, shout—long live the king and set him on his (David's) throne. David told them to declare that he had appointed Solomon as king in his place. Of course, they followed the king's instructions. When Adonijah heard that King

David had made Solomon king, he became afraid and took hold of the horns of the altar. He refused to leave the altar until Solomon promised that he would not put him to death. Solomon said that if he would show himself worthy, he would not touch him, but if he is found doing evil, he would surely die. Soon after that Adonijah asked Bathsheba to ask Solomon for Abishag the beautiful young Shunamite woman that was given to David at the end of his life to care for him as his companion. Solomon was insulted at Adonijah's request, and he had him put to death.

Micah, Abigail and Bathsheba were wives of David. They played very important roles in David's life as well as making sure that God's plan was carried out. They risked their lives to see to it that others were saved and in some cases that their own lives were saved. They were women whose names and life stories were written in the Bible to be remembered forever as heroes. They were women who chose to follow God's ways rather than man's ways; therefore, we can see the difference they made.

The Widow at Zarephath

In the conclusion of women that God used in the Old Testament Scriptures, it would not be fitting not to mention the widow at Zarephath who obeyed the Prophet Elijah. There was a horrible famine in the land, the brook that was supplying Elijah's water dried up. Then God told him to go to Zarephath right away because He had commanded a widow there to feed him. So Elijah went and found a widow at the town gate gathering sticks. He asked her to please bring him a little jar of water and a piece of bread. The woman told him that as surely as the LORD lives, she did not have any bread—only a handful of flour and a little oil in a jug. She went on further and told him that she was gathering the sticks to take home and make the last meal for her and her son. Then there was nothing else to do but die.

Elijah told the woman to not be afraid, to go home, and do as she had said. But she was to make a small cake of bread for him first and take it to him. Then she was to make something for herself and her son.

"For this is what the LORD, the God of Israel, says: 'The jar of flour will not be used up and the jug of oil will not run dry until the day the LORD gives rain on the land' (I Kings 17:14, NIV)." Of course the woman obeyed the prophet and the prophecy was set in motion. She did not run out of flour or oil. While everyone else was starving, she, her son and the prophet Elijah had bread to eat.

But that was not the only miracle that God gave the widow, her son became very ill and died. The widow said to Prophet Elijah, **"What do you have against me, man of God? Did you come to remind me of my sin and kill my son (Kings 17:18, NIV)?"** Elijah asked her to give the boy's lifeless body to him. He carried him upstairs to the room that he stayed in and laid him on his bed. Then he cried out in prayer to the LORD asking Him to let the boy's life return to him. The LORD answered his prayer, and life came back into the boy. Elijah carried the living child downstairs and gave him to his mother. The woman told Elijah that the experience they had just come through not only proved but sealed the fact in her mind that he was a man of God with the word of God in his mouth that was the truth.

When we examine the character of this woman, we can see that she had a relationship with God due to the fact that she put her trust in the Prophet Elijah's words. Most importantly, we also know that she had a relationship with God, because God told Elijah to go to Zarephath to find her. I Kings 17: 9 states that God told Elijah that He had commanded a widow there to supply his food. She also provided him with a room in the upper part of her house. So, the LORD saw to it that the widow was provided for and at the same time, the prophet was being provided for as well. If the widow had been selfish and not obeyed the prophet, she and her son would have starved to death. But, because she knew that she should put her hope and faith in God, she acted by faith, and God honored her according to her act of obedient.

Another Widow

In II Kings 4, there is a story about another widow who cried out to the prophet Elisha. She told him that her husband who was from a company of prophets had died. The widow reminded Elisha that he knew her husband and that he knew that he loved and revered the LORD. She went on further to say that her husband's creditor was coming soon to take her two sons to be his slaves. Elisha asked her what he could do to help her. Then he asked her what does she have in her house? She told him that she had nothing except a little oil. Elisha told her to go to her neighbors and borrow as many jars as she could, not just a few but many. Then she was to go inside her house along with her sons and close the door. He told her to pour the oil into all of the jars. When she filled one, she was to set it aside and fill the next jar until they were all full. She borrowed the jars just as the prophet told her to do. The widow began to pour and the oil did not stop flowing until she had no more jars to fill. She went to Elisha and told him that she had filled all the jars that she borrowed. Elisha told her to go sell the oil and pay off her creditor. Then she and her sons could live off of what was left over.

This widow reminded God of her husband's faithfulness, respect and love for Him. Evidently, she knew God and had seen God do wonders, because her husband was a prophet that kept company with Elisha and other prophets. So, the woman knew that God could and would provide; therefore, she went to the man of God and asked him to tell her how to get God to move on her behalf. Elisha knew the woman, and he knew what she said was true. He did not hesitate to speak directions to her that would solve her problem.

The very valuable lesson that is seen in this story is that we need to seek God's help and directions when we are in a crisis or have problems and cannot see our way out. Sometimes it may mean that we need to find a true man or woman of God, one that really practice living according to the Word, to ask for help or advice. Sometimes we can go directly to God in worship and in prayer, and He will answer us with provision for whatever we need. The Book of James states that we have not, because we ask not. Just like this widow woman, we should know who to go to when we need help.

A Shunammite Woman

In the same chapter of II Kings, Elisha met a woman in Shunem, who invited him to dinner; she was a woman with wealth. Afterward, whenever he went to and by that town, he would stop at her house to eat with her and her husband. The woman told her husband that she knew that Elisha was a holy man of God. She asked her husband to build a small room on their roof for him to stay whenever he came to their house. They built the room and placed a bed, a table, a chair and a lamp in it for Elisha, and he stayed in it as often as he visited.

One day while the man of God was lying in his room, he told his servant Gehazi to call in the Shunammite woman. When she came in and stood before him, he asked her what could he do for her, since she had gone to all the trouble to provide a place for him and Gehazi to stay. She told him that she had a home among her people; therefore, she was content. So, Elisha asked Gehazi what gift he thought would be fitting and pleasing for her. Gehazi's answer was that she had no son and that her husband was old. Elisha told Gehazi to call her again. This time Elisha told her that **"About this time next year, you will hold a son in your arms (II Kings 4:16, NIV)."** The woman became pregnant and gave birth to a son about the same time of the next year.

One day after the child was older; he went out to his father in the field, who was with the reapers. He complained to his father that his head was hurting badly. He told one of the servants to take him to his mother. The servant lifted him up and carried him to his mother. His mother held him on her lap until noon, and then he died. She took him up to the prophet room, laid him on Elisha's bed and closed the door behind her. Then she called her husband and asked him to please send her a servant and a donkey for her to go to the man of God and return quickly. Of course, her husband asked her why she needed to go to see the man of God. But, she told him that it was all right.

The Shunammite woman went to where the man of God was, and Elisha recognized her from a distant while she was on her way to reach him. When she reached him, she fell at his feet and told him what had happened to her son. Elisha sent his servant Gehazi ahead of them to lay his staff on the child's face. Gehazi did as he was asked and on his way back he met Elisha and the child's mother on their way to the child. He reported to the man of God that the child did not awaken when he laid the staff on his face. When Elisha reached the house, he went into his room where the boy was lying and closed the door with him only being in the room with the boy. First, he prayed. Then he got on the bed and stretched himself out upon the boy's body, and the boy's body became warm. Elisha did this twice while praying to God. The second time that he was upon the boy's body, the boy sneezed seven times and opened his eyes. Then Elisha called in the woman and Gehazi. After the woman came in and saw that her son was alive, she fell at the prophet's feet in gratefulness. Then she took her son in her arms and left the room.

Wow! What an awesome life to live ministering to the prophet. The Shunammite woman experienced God's favor, because she took care of the man of God whenever he came into their town. God gave her two miracles: a child and his resurrection from the dead all because she knew what God could do, and she knew that he would do it through the man of God.

This is why everyone should have a true man or woman of God to cover them. Today, there are too many men and women of God who may have started out sincere, but somehow have gotten off track and somewhere lost their way. They have succumbed to the idea that they are great by the means of the world. God has lifted the precious anointing off of them just as he did Saul, because they do not listen to God; they listen to man and their own selfish hearts which are contrary to the Word of God. This fact is evident because God's power and His backing are not demonstrated through signs, wonders and miracles in their ministry. Some have been able to maintain what looks like true ministry, but that is only due to people faith in God and their strong belief that God can and will perform miracles. Carnal minded Christians are becoming more wide spread, and the true Word of God is not practiced like it should be; therefore, very few people are experiencing miracles.

On the other hand, there are still many Christians who do believe and practice the true Word of God. They are considered to be the true worshippers that John 4: 24 speaks about. God looks at the heart of people: therefore, He knows who the real Christians are and who are not real. People who practice real Christianity are the true worshippers who experience the miracles all the time, because not all miracles are as big as someone being raised from the dead.

The widow at Zarephath, the other widow and the Shunammite woman all received God's favor because their hearts were right and their faith in God was strong. They showed God that they were all about pleasing Him through their obedience to the men of God that He sent their way. God in turn blessed them beyond measure or reason. In other words, there was no logical reason why they were blessed the way that they were blessed. He blessed them with abundant. God provided enough for them to take care of them for the rest of their lives which caused them to be care free and fulfilled. He is a *GREAT GOD!*

Chapter 11

Elizabeth

In the New Testament, Elizabeth and her husband Zechariah are introduced in Luke 1: 5. Their story ends at the end of the chapter. Elizabeth was a descendant of Aaron along with her husband which meant that she was born into the tribe of the Levites who were the family of priests that God established in the Old Testament. Both she and her husband were righteous in the Lord's sight, because they always kept his commandments and ordinances. The beginning of the New Testament marks the time to bring John and Jesus into the world. John had to be born first, because he was the forerunner for Jesus. God needed a woman who would be qualified and who would obey him.

God chose Elizabeth to be the one who would have the privilege of being John's mother. She was a woman who had gotten up in age and who had no children. Gabriel, the messenger angel appeared to Zechariah in the temple and told him that he and his wife would have a son. He told him to name him John, and he told him that his son would be a delight and a joy to him. Many would be happy because of John's birth due to the fact that he would be great in the sight of the Lord. Gabriel informed Zechariah that his son was never to drink wine or any fermented drink. He said that he would be filled with the Holy Spirit even in his mother's womb from birth; therefore, he would bring back many of the Israelites to the Lord their God. According to Luke 1:17 John would **"go on before the Lord, in the Spirit and power of Elijah, to turn the hearts of the fathers to their children**

and the disobedient to the wisdom of the righteous—to make ready a people prepared for the Lord (NIV)."

Zechariah asked the angel questions which caused Gabriel to make him dumb. In other words, he could not speak until John was born. He asked the angel, how could he be sure of what Gabriel was telling him. By making Zachariah dumb, Gabriel was telling him in a sense that he stands in the presence of God and takes his orders directly from God. He made him to be not able to ask another question that would create doubt, because doubt can sometime destroy a seed. Elizabeth certainly did not need to hear any doubt from him.

After Elizabeth became pregnant, she stayed hidden away in seclusion for five months. She was rejoicing, because she felt that God had shown her favor and took away her disgrace. In those times, women felt that the biggest part of being a woman was to be able to have children and care for them. Having children gave them a sense of accomplishment and worth. Many women today still have these feelings. Since Elizabeth had gotten up in age, she probably thought that she would never have a child and that everyone looked down on her as if something was wrong with her. But now she knew that God himself had done something so very special and wonderful just for her. He had favored her. Not only did He bless her to have a child, but He blessed her to rear one of the most important men in New Testament Bible history.

I believe Elizabeth stayed in seclusion for five months in order to protect the seed that she was carrying from negative words that people would speak concerning her and the baby. Zechariah had already been stricken dumb because of doubt, and I am sure that Elizabeth did not want to hear what people had to say about the matter until they could see with their physical eyes that she was carrying a baby. Also, during the first trimester or the first three months of pregnancy is a very crucial, critical time. Usually, it is during this stage that miscarriages or abortions happen. Since we know that Satan works to trick the minds through thoughts and suggestions presented to it, he would have loved nothing more than to plant seed of doubt and unbelief in

Elizabeth's mind which could have caused her to possibly abort her seed.

I can identify with this logic due to my first two pregnancies ended in miscarriages. I lost them within the first six to eight weeks of pregnancy. I often felt that I announced my pregnancies too soon. When I became pregnant the third time, my husband at that time and I agreed not to tell anyone until I was past the first trimester. The third pregnancy was a success, and today, he continues to be a delightful success.

Elizabeth knew God intimately already which was why God chose her. She probably lived to please God all of her life after all, she was born into the family who duties and callings were to minister unto the Lord as priests and servants of the temple. Elizabeth showed God her heart by keeping His commandments and ordinances blamelessly according the Bible. God saw her daily and was evidently pleased with her. So, He chose her and entrusted her to bring John, the forerunner—the one to go before Jesus and prepare the way for him into the world. Elizabeth and her husband had to be people who listen to God and who would carry out his commandments; because God wanted John reared a certain way.

Also, Elizabeth was so in tune with God that she prophesied and spoke words of encouragement to Mary during her time of pregnancy. She displayed her humbleness when she honored Mary by the way she spoke to her and by the things she said to her. Elizabeth spoke of God's favor towards her, because she felt honored that Mary the mother of the Lord Jesus came to see her. The wisdom and knowledge of God were displayed through her because she knew that Mary was carrying God's only begotten son. Elizabeth was filled with the Holy Spirit when Mary greeted her. There was a very strong spirit of agreement between the two spirit beings that were developing inside of them.

The Bible says that Gabriel, the angel only spoke to Zechariah and told him to name his son John. But when the time came to name him, Elizabeth said that his name was John. The people must have opposed her strongly, because they went to Zechariah and asked him what the baby's name was. Then Zechariah's speech came back to him, and he said the same name that Elizabeth had said. It seemed strange that the people were not going to take Elizabeth's word in naming her son. They persisted in pursuing Zechariah to ask him if that was what he wanted to name his son. They probably would have named their baby Zachariah if he would not have spoken up. The people treated Elizabeth as though her thought, opinion, or idea did not matter. It was if she really had no say so. After all, John was the baby that she had just given birth too, but that fact did not matter to them. They looked to Zechariah for something different than what his wife was saying. Unfortunately, women and sometimes men allow themselves to walk out of God's will by listening to people and following their advice. The funny thing about the whole situation is that the people should not have had any opinion or any authority in the matter anyway. They certainly should not have gone to Elizabeth's husband to try to get him to contradict what she said, but that is exactly what they did. These were their friends and possibly their family members. But thank God, Zechariah and Elizabeth had a relationship with God which allowed them to have an agreement with each other and God. They knew what their son's name was, and in agreement they put a stop to the devil's madness.

God looked for a woman when it was time to introduce John into the world, a woman who would obey him. He found that woman in Elizabeth who possessed all the qualities that He was looking for to train and shape John into the person that he became. God found her worthy, and He equipped her for her special assignment. Because she was accustomed to doing what God asked her to do, her assignment was easy and pleasing to her. It was delightful and brought her great joy. Elizabeth was the best choice to be John, the Baptist mother. She obeyed the Lord willingly. God is still observing and looking for women like Elizabeth today.

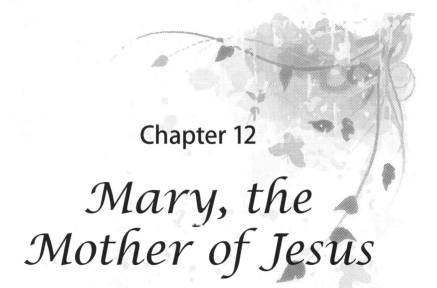

Chapter 12

Mary, the Mother of Jesus

As we move on through the Scripture, we find the next woman that God used mightily. She first appeared in the middle of Elizabeth's story in Luke 1. As a matter of fact, she was Elizabeth's cousin and her divine assignment from God was directly connected to Elizabeth's divine assignment. Again, God looked for a woman, a very very special extraordinary woman. This woman did not fit in the category of just any woman. She topped the scale when godly characteristics were weighed among women. No, she was no ordinary woman. This woman was favored by God because of the life she lived by being humbled and obedient to God's Word.

When the angel, Gabriel met with her, he told her that ***she was highly favored by God and the Lord was with her.*** Because she was troubled by what the angel had said to her, he told her that she had found favor with God. Elizabeth said to her that she was blessed because she believed what God told her through the angel. Even the woman described herself as being a humble servant in Luke 1 in a song that she sang beginning in verse 46.

Since Gabriel told this woman that she had found favor with God and was highly favored by God, it became clear that God had looked for a woman. The word find (found) indicates that someone is looking for something. But why wouldn't God look for the best possible woman to be the mother of his only begotten Son? This woman's name was Mary. She was a young virgin girl. The word *virgin means pure, uncorrupted, not hitherto used or processed and never had sexual intercourse* according to <u>Webster's Standard Dictionary</u>. Mary possessed all of the qualities that God needed a human woman to have. She was the woman in whom God told Satan (the serpent) about in Genesis 3:15 when he told him that he would use the woman's offspring to crush his head. It was time for that offspring or some call him, the woman's seed to come into the earth; therefore, God found the purest vessel in a woman that he could find.

It was obviously that Mary had a serious relationship with God, because the angel said the Lord was with her. Also, she believed what the angel said about what would happen to her. Since she was Elizabeth's cousin, this indicates that she was probably in the Levites family too which made her a minister to God from birth. She knew his commandments and ordinances and kept them. But God looks at the heart of a person. The attitude of the heart toward him is very important. Evidently, when He looked at Mary, He saw a pure heart that carried all of the attributes that are found in the fruit of the Spirit. He saw a right attitude toward Him, a servant's attitude. Mary was pleased to serve Him. She did not serve Him out of a sense of duty and obligation; she served Him willingly and with pleasure.

Whenever Gabriel appeared until a person, he came with a message and an assignment from God to him/her. The message or assignment to Mary was that the Holy Ghost would overshadow her, and she would conceive a child. Mary did not question her assignment. She did not doubt whether the angel was telling her the truth or not. She simply said to Gabriel, **"I am the Lord's servant. May it be to me as you have said (Luke 1:38, NIV)."** In other words, she said here I am Lord. I am your servant. You may use me anyway that you want to use me. I belong to you anyway. I am a willing vessel that is glad and honored to be used by you. By Mary having the attitude of a humble servant and by her surrendering her will unto the Lord, it is easy to see why she was favored above all women.

Mary did not let Satan bombard her mind with 'what if' thoughts. She did not get caught up in thinking about herself and what others would say about her, because in the natural it looked like Mary had been sexually active but was not married. This little fact did not stop her from accepting the assignment that God was giving her. This time God could not use man in this situation. This equation only required God and woman. All other births require God, man and woman in order for them to become reality. But Mary probably did not consider that she would be ridiculed and mocked at nor did she think about the shame that she could have been made to feel. Her thoughts and desires were only to be used by God and to please Him.

Mary never complained when the circumstances around her did not look good. When it was time for her to deliver the baby, she had to deliver in a stable with cows and other livestock, she did not say 'why me, of all people.' Mary never boasted about the fact that God chose her over all other women. She remained humble and obedient to God throughout her whole assignment. Because when a child is born, he becomes the parents' responsibility for life.

Mary's son was and is the most important human that had and has ever walked on the face of the earth. She, besides her husband was probably the only human that really knew who Jesus was in the beginning. Mary did not take lightly her responsibility as a mother to her child; even though, she knew he was deity. The times that Mary is seen in the Scriptures was in Luke 2 when she gave birth to Jesus; again when she and Joseph took him to the temple to present him to the Lord; and yet again when Jesus was twelve years old and was left in Jerusalem.

Mary never called attention to herself or Jesus; although God displayed a glorious presentation of His son's birth. Because when Jesus was born God put a bright shining star in the sky that was seen from far and near. It was such a wonder that shepherds and kings followed for the purpose of seeing the holy child that was born and to bring him gifts. Wow! Look at God announcing his son's birth as a proud father and look at Him providing earthly goods and provisions for him! It was said that the gifts that were given to Jesus were enough to provide for him for all of his life on earth. *What an AWESOME GOD!* His mother did not announce that her son was also the living god that the Scripture that prophesied his coming was talking about in the Old Testament. Most women would have not been able to contain themselves with all of the miraculous things happening to them. But, Mary remained quiet and humble about all of it.

Being a new mother with the scary responsibilities of doing all the right things for a baby, Mary had to stay in relationship to her baby's father, God. Since God Himself knew that Mary and Joseph would obey him because they loved him, He ordered their footsteps. When the time came to take Jesus to the temple to present him to the LORD, God had the righteous and devout people in place to speak blessings over him. They both knew who Jesus was. Simeon, a devout and righteous man, was waiting to see the Christ. He was an old man, but it had been revealed to him by the Holy Spirit that he would not die until he saw the Christ. He took Jesus the Christ into his arms, prophesied over him and blessed him. He also prophesied to Mary that ***"her son would cause the falling and rising of many in Israel, and to be a sign that will be spoken against, so that the thoughts of many hearts will be revealed. And a sword will pierce her own soul too (Luke 2:34-35, NIV)."***

Then Anna, also a prophetess and very old, gave thanks and spoke about the child to all who were looking forward to the redemption of Jerusalem. Anna lived in the temple for many years. She lived with her husband for seven years after they were married. He died and she became a widow. At the time that Joseph and Mary brought Jesus to the temple to be blessed as a baby, Anna was then eighty-four years old. After becoming a widow, she never left the temple. Anna spent all of her time worshipping God—night and day, fasting and praying. She was someone that God was very familiar with. Also, God knew that she was one of the best choices of people to lay hands on Jesus and speak blessings over him. So, God sent Joseph and Mary to look for the best two people who carried His anointing to bless His Only Begotten Son.

Notice God did not allow just any old body to pray over and bless his son. He chose devout righteous people that were living in obedience to Him. It is funny that men and women want to pray for others but are not living the kind of life that God requires them to live. They do not possess the will to live righteous and do not seem to make any effort to do right. They display ungodly lives before others without appearing to even be embarrassed about how they conduct themselves in their everyday living. They are unrighteous. Unrighteous people certainly do not need to pray or prophesy for anyone else. They cannot speak God's blessings over others when they do not know the will of God for themselves. They cannot really know Him and be ungodly.

When Jesus was twelve years old, his parents had to go to Jerusalem for the Feast of Passover according to custom. On their way back home and after traveling for a day, Mary and Joseph realized that they had left Jesus behind, because they looked for him among all of their relatives and the company of people that were traveling with them. When they returned to Jerusalem, it had been three days to find Jesus. When they found him, he was in the temple courts, sitting among the teachers, listening to them and asking them questions. Everyone who heard his understanding and answers were amazed and astonished, including his parents. Mary asked him why he treated them that way. Jesus' answer was, why was she searching for him? Then he asked, **"Didn't you know I had to be in my Father's house (Luke 2:49, NIV)?"** After that incident, Jesus went to Nazareth with his parents and was obedient to them. Mary treasured all the things that had been spoken over him and all the things that he had done in her heart.

I can relate to the horrible feelings that Mary must have had when she did not know where Jesus was. When my youngest child was around two years old, I lost him for a few minutes. I was at our local city mall inside of Dillard's looking at all the different merchandizes. I had my baby by the hand as we walked around. I stopped in the ladies' department and moved a few dresses on one of the dress racks. In the process of handling the dresses, I let go of my baby's hand. When I stopped looking at the dresses, I reached down for my son's hand who I thought was standing right beside me, but he was not there. I could not see him anywhere. As a matter of fact, there was no one around not even a store employee. I called out his name several times, each time louder, but he did not answer nor appear. First, I turned frantically around in circles with my eyes searching up and down aisles in the store to see where my baby could have wondered off to. My heart began to beat faster and louder. I could feel the blood rushing around into all parts of my body especially my head. I remember catching my head and asking myself what should I do. Thoughts began to flood my mind; someone took your baby without you seeing him. My baby was friendly and possibly would not have cried if someone picked him up and walked off with him. By that time, my head began to feel like it was going to explode, and my heart felt as if it was going to jump out of my chest. Suddenly, the thought came to go to the mall's office and have an announcement made about my son's where about over the intercom. Just when I started to make a step toward the office, it was if I could not move. I felt paralyzed being torn between not wanting to leave the spot where I last saw my baby in case he was nearby and wanting to leave to make the announce in case someone was trying to leave the mall with him. Then the Holy Spirit said to me calming, 'calm down, take a deep breath and look down.' I looked down, and there was my baby stooping down under another rack of dresses hiding from me. I began to cry and thank God. When his eyes met mine, he came from under the dress rack to me. I picked him up, kissed him and hugged him tightly. Then I told him firmly not to ever do that again to me.

I was horrified by this incident which probably lasted no more than two to three minutes if that long. I can imagine that Mary's three days experience of not knowing where her son was must have been pure hell. Satan probably had a good time tantalizing her with thoughts of the worse possible scenarios that could have happened. She probably thought that she was a terrible mother for letting her son out of her eye sight. I had that thought. It may have seemed that Jesus got smart with his mother when she asked him why he had treated her that way, but I am sure that by him reminding her who his father was, he was assuring her that his father (God) was taking care of him, and she should not have been worried. After all, Mary had a rhema word directly from God about him. She knew that she could count on God to protect her son.

Mary pondered and treasured things in her heart about Jesus which means that she thought about and meditated on what she had heard and seen. Mary held things as a treasure in her heart about Jesus. Mary was no different from any other mother when it came to being a loving nurturing mother to her child, but she is a prime example of what a mother should be like. Every mother should know who their children are to a certain degree. No, God did not send Gabriel to every mother to tell them who their child would be before conception, but things are prophesied and said about children that mothers should take notice of. Some things that are said about children should be rejected by mothers, because it is mothers' duty to see to it that their child is protected against the devil's schemes that are placed in their paths to destroy them. On the other hand, mothers should take careful consideration of all the good things that are said about their children, because we look for ways to help shape our children into successful productive citizens. For example, if it has been prophesied that a child would be a mighty man of God, then it is the parent's responsibility to train that child up in the things of God. He should be taught the Word of God from a very young age just like Samuel was trained. But, every mother should train their children in the Word of God anyway.

Mary is seen next in John 2. Mary showed that she was a very compassionate woman when she offered a solution to the problem that the host of a wedding had when he ran out of wine during the wedding party. Since she knew without a shadow of doubt who her son was, she offered him as a problem solver to the host's servants. Mary told Jesus that there was no more wine. Jesus said to her, **"Dear woman, why do you involve me? My time has not yet come (John 2:4, NIV)."** His mother turned to the servants and said to them, **"Do whatever he tells you."** Then Jesus instructed the servants to fill the six huge stone water pots that were there. After the pots were filled, he told them to draw some out and take it to the master of the banquet. Of course, the master's comment was that the best wine was saved until the banquet was just about to end. Mary through Jesus had saved the host the embarrassment of not having enough wine to accommodate his guests.

The last time that Mary is seen in the Scripture communicating with Jesus is in John 19. Jesus looked down and saw his mother standing near the cross while he was being crucified. Mary was helplessly grieving the crucifixion of her baby boy. Jesus saw the pain on her face and in her heart. Then he saw John, the disciple that he loved, and he said to his mother, **"Dear woman, here is your son (John 19:26, NIV)."** He said to the disciple, **"Here is your mother (John 19: 27, NIV),"** and the disciple immediately took Mary to his home. I could never or would ever want to imagine what she must have been feeling during those last hours of Jesus' earthly life. Jesus had compassion for her and sent her away with John to keep her from watching him in his darkest hour. Mary probably understood more than anyone that the cross was Jesus' destiny, but it still must have been very agonizing and painful for her to watch her son's crucifixion and death. However, Mary was depicted as a very kind and compassionated woman. She was a woman that was happy to please God; therefore, Jesus displayed not only his father's characteristics but his mother's too. Mary was the one, who birth him, nurtured and cared for him, taught and trained him, and shaped him in an earthly fashion. It was easy for her to pass on God's characteristics to her son, because after all Mary displayed the attributes of God herself. That is why God chose her to be the mother of His only begotten son.

Most people believe that Mary is considered to be the single most important woman in the history of mankind. Some religions treat her as deity. This was due to the fact that God teamed up with her to bring the most important human being there is into the earth, Jesus Christ, our Lord and Savior. They feel that only deity can birth deity; therefore, Mary had to be deity too, because she is the mother of Jesus. He came through her body and was reared under her loving care. These religions honor Mary and pray to her as the mother of Jesus just as they pray to God, the father of Jesus. God said that He would use a woman to bring forth a seed that would bruise the Devil's (serpent's) head, and he did just that through Mary. We know that when God spoke the punishment to the serpent, he was not just talking about Jesus. All of mankind fit into the prophecy of whatever was spoken. All men, women and serpents live under the curses, but Jesus was the perfect seed that had to come to set the president and make the prophecy legal. Adam started out perfect, but he failed. Jesus did not fail; therefore, God is still somewhat pleased with his creation. Eve is very important, because she is the first woman and the first mother. The process of reproduction began with Eve and Adam. There was but one order in which babies could be conceived and brought into the earth, but God changed the conception process when He sent Jesus into the world. He took man out of the process and used only a woman whose name was Mary, a humble God loving and God fearing woman. No matter what the belief is concerning Mary, everyone should to be thankful that God found the kind of woman that He was looking for to bring our Savior into the earth. Everyone should thank God for Mary, the mother of Jesus.

Chapter 13

The Samaritan Woman

One day during Jesus' ministry on the earth, he had to go through Samaria on his way back to Galilee. He had been in Judea. Because he was tired, he sat by Jacob's well, which was built by Jacob during his life time, in the town of Sychar in Samaria. Jesus was sitting at the well alone. His disciples who were traveling with him had gone into the town to buy food. A Samaritan woman came to the well to get water, and Jesus saw her. He asked her to give him a drink. The Samaritan woman said to him, **"You are a Jew, and I am a Samaritan woman. How can you ask me for a drink? (For Jews do not associate with Samaritans.)"** Then Jesus said, **"If you knew the gift of God and who it is that asks you for a drink, you would have asked him and he would have given you living water (John 4:9-10, NIV)."** As they continued to talked, Jesus offered the woman salvation. She asked Jesus to give her the water that he spoke about so she would not ever thirst again.

Then Jesus asked her to go and bring back her husband. She told him that she had no husband. Jesus said to her that she had told him the truth, because she had had five husbands, and the husband that she was with then or presently was not hers. The woman said to him that she could see that he was a prophet. She then began to question him about where people should worship God. The woman told him that her forefathers believed that they should worship God in the mountains, but the Jews believe that He should be worshipped in Jerusalem. She asked Jesus which one was correct in their belief. Jesus told her that salvation is from the Jews and that the Samaritans worship what they do not know, but the Jews worship what they do know. Then he told her that the time is coming and has now come when worship to God will no longer take place in Jerusalem or on a mountain. God seeks true worshippers, and because God is spirit, they that worship Him must worship in spirit and in truth. Then the woman stated, **"I know that Messiah (called Christ) is coming. When he comes, he will explain everything to us (John 4:25, NIV)."** Then Jesus revealed to her that he was the Christ. He told her that he was the one that she was speaking about.

The woman went back into town and immediately began to tell everyone about her encounter with a man that told her all about her life. She urged the people to go and see the man. The people went to him and begged him to stay with them for a while. Jesus stayed in Samaria for two days speaking words to them, and because of his words many became believers. Then the people told the woman that because they heard Jesus for themselves, they no longer had to believe because of her words. They said that they knew that Jesus really was the Savior of the world.

This passage of Scripture is found in John 4. The significance of this story is that Jesus went through Samaria but stopped for a while first to minister to a woman who compelled others to come to him. Then he was able to minister to many in that town perhaps the entire region of Samaritans. Jesus looked for or maybe he was destined to come into contact with the Samaritan woman. Again, just as the angels appeared to women in the past, this time Jesus appeared to this woman, and he told her things that caused her to know that he was someone very special in God and with God. Because only a person who knows God in a personal way can prophesy to people that they did not know things that are true about themselves. Jesus told this woman things that she was not proud of and probably things that she tried to hide from others. He went into her secret place, her closet immediately and spoke directly about her problems. He revealed to her that he knew her problems and that if she chose to be delivered, her deliverance could only come through him.

The Samaritan woman undoubtedly got a very serious revelation when she came into the presence of Jesus, because she accepted his offer of freedom from the bondage that she was living under. Jesus told this woman that she had five husbands and the one that she was with was not her own. Since he said that she had husbands, it is logical to assume that she had been sleeping with other women's husbands. In other words, she was a reproach to society, a home wrecker and an adulteress prostitute. By law she could have been stoned to death if she was caught with one of the husbands. So, she probably lived a very secluded life away from the rest of the people. Evidently, she went to the well by herself when no one else was there to avoid being among others; therefore, she had to be living with shame and fear. The woman should have been afraid of being caught eventually, because one can only hide sin for a short while. My mother often says that sin done in the dark always comes to the light. After Jesus told her the things that she had been trying to hide from others, she must have felt that she had been caught. Jesus made it clear to her that she could not hide anything from God, and if God wanted to reveal her doings, He could and He did. Then the woman understood that she had been seen by the most high God and that she needed to do something to break free of the chains that were holding her in bondage. She surrendered her life to him and accepted the freedom that he offered her.

After the woman received the kind of contact that you get when you accept Jesus into your heart for the first time, she had to go and tell someone. She could not keep what she had just experienced to herself. The woman wanted the world to know what Jesus had done for her. He lifted a very heavy burden off of her. She felt so free that she did not think about herself or the acts that she had been committing. Those acts became a past that she was happy to leave behind. She only thought about what she was feeling in the moment. The woman was feeling peace, love and joy in the Holy Spirit, because the Holy Spirit was what she had just received. She felt accepted and loved. So, she went back into town with a message, a testimony, which pointed to Jesus. Evidently, she had some influence with some of the people, because people went to Jesus after she told them to come and see the man.

I believe that Jesus was such a man of destiny that all of his actions were done in order to get results for the kingdom of God. All of his footsteps were ordered by God, and every meeting that he had with people had a specific, divine purpose. The woman asked Jesus when they first spoke, why he was talking to her. She asked him the question because the Samarians and the Jews had different opinions about where they should worship God; therefore, they did not associate with each other. Since, she pointed out to Jesus that He was a Jew; it was obvious that the Samarians did not converse with Jews. Jesus, on the other hand, was a man of purpose, so he continued to talk to her. The woman probably did not get much conversation from the Samaritans either due to her lifestyle. But Jesus' focus was on giving her the opportunity to be delivered and then her helping to bring others into their deliverance. After all, Jesus main purpose for coming into the earth was that mankind would be saved, all of mankind not just Jewish people but all people. At that particular time Jesus was waiting for that woman, because not only did He know that she was in need of deliverance, but He also knew that she would be His connection to get to many of the Samaritans. This woman answer yes to the Lord when He called her, and God used her to evangelize her town, because she went to the streets and the byways and compelled the people to come and see the man who told her all about herself. Through her willingness to be used by God and her actions to tell people about Jesus many believed.

Chapter 14

Other Women whom Jesus Blessed

During Jesus' ministry on earth, he encountered and interacted with several women who he blessed, saved, and delivered. This chapter will simply mention some of them. Most of these women were not given names; they were identified by their problem or by their nationality. Their stories left a legacy for the world to read and gain faith from, but their names do not matter. The message and the power of God remain the same. If Jesus saved and delivered them in the past, then he will save and deliver us today. Our God does not change. He is the same yesterday, today and forever; He is no respecter of persons. Most of these accounts, stories or testimonies were written in all four of the Gospel Books in the Bible: Matthew, Mark, Luke, and John. All four authors testified that these incidents, which were miracles, actually happened. There were a few that only one or two authors wrote about, but their stories were still worth telling.

Jesus showed his love and compassion for women everywhere he went. In the Books of Matthew, Mark, and Luke, the authors wrote about Jesus going into Simon Peter's house and finding his mother-in-law in bed sick with a fever. He touched her and healed her. All three authors said that Jesus took hold of her hand and helped her up out of the bed. Then she immediately, that very moment, got up and began to wait on and serve them. Evidently, Peter's mother-in-law must have been too sick to even get out of bed. The first thing that Jesus did when he entered her house was healed her. Since Jesus is deity and knows no illness within his own body, the illness could not stay in his presence anyway. So when Jesus, the healer, came to her house her sickness had to leave.

In Luke 7, Luke described to us a picture of Jesus as a very loving, caring, and compassionate man. Jesus met a funeral procession on his way into a town called Nain, and he saw a mother who was a widow getting ready to bury her only son. He was moved in his heart, and his heart went out to her. Jesus said to her, **"Don't cry."** Then he touched the coffin and said, **"Young man, I say to you, get up (Luke 7:14, NIV)!"** The young man sat up and began to talk. Then Jesus gave him back to his mother. Here we see Jesus empathizing with a mother whose heart was broken. Jesus had so much compassion for her that he could not stand to see her grieving any longer; therefore, He brought her son back from the dead and gave him back to his mother. The young man was presented to her by Jesus as a gift of his love and kindness.

In John 7 and 8, John wrote about a woman that was brought to Jesus while he was in the temple court teaching a group of people who had gathered around him. The Pharisees and the teachers of the law brought this woman to Jesus. They made her stand before the people, and they told Jesus that she had been caught in the act of adultery. Then they told Jesus that the Law Moses wrote commanded them to stone her to death. They asked for Jesus' opinion, because they wanted to find something to accuse him of. But Jesus bent down and wrote on the ground with his finger. The Pharisees and teachers of the law kept questioning him. After a few moments, Jesus straightened up his body into a standing position and said to them, **"If any one of you is without sin, let him be the first to throw a stone at her (John 8:7, NIV)."** Then he stooped down and continued to write on the ground. After hearing what he said the people began to leave one at a time until they were all gone. The older people left first; Jesus and the woman were the only ones left there. Jesus stood up straight and asked her, was there anyone left to condemn her. She said to him, **"No one, sir."** Then Jesus declared to her, **"Neither do I condemn you. Go now and leave your life of sin (John 8:11, NIV)."**

In this story, we see Jesus showing a woman mercy by showing the Pharisees and teachers of the law that they were not without sin. It has been said that Jesus probably was writing some of the sins that they committed and possibly were still committing when he was writing on the ground with his finger. Wow, it must have been an eye opener for them to see how Jesus responded to their questions and their foolishness. Because it was foolish to bring the woman who was caught in the very act but did not bring the man. That almost looks like a half truth or lie. It also has been said that maybe one of them was the man. Nevertheless, Jesus who is like his Father in heaven knows all; therefore, why wouldn't he point their sins out to them. They obviously knew that he knew that they were not without sin; so, they left when Jesus asked them to examine themselves. I wonder how many of them had committed a sin that required stoning according to the Law.

Jesus was compassionated toward this woman; so he gave her a second chance. He gave her a second chance to make things right in her life and to live a life free of willfully sinning. The very fact that this woman came in contact with Jesus gave her an edge in life. Just like the woman at the well also known as the Samaritan woman, this woman was given the opportunity to drink of the water that had the power to cause her to never thirst again. This woman is not mentioned in the Bible any more after this short passage of Scripture. It is not known whether or not she did like the woman at the well and ran told everyone to come see a man. But one thing is for sure, her story is used to teach a valuable lesson to all of mankind, which is no one is sinless, and if everyone would examine themselves, he or she would not have time or the heart to examine anyone else. Because when we earnestly look at self, we see unrighteous things in us that will take a lifetime to rid ourselves of; therefore we would not have time to persecute our fellowman or woman.

In Luke 13:10, Jesus healed a woman who had been crippled by a spirit for eighteen years. Jesus noticed her while he was teaching in one of the synagogues on the Sabbath day; she was bent over and could not straighten up. Jesus called her to him and touched her. He said to her that she was set free from her infirmity. Immediately the woman straightened up and began praising God. Jesus is still looking at us. He is still moved with compassion for us. He still heals today, because he is our redeemer. He loves us and wants to make us whole by healing us of all of our diseases and sicknesses.

Jesus saw these women, but there were other women who sought after him and got his attention such as the woman with the issue of blood, the Canaanite woman, and the woman with the alabaster box. These women had unwavering faith in Jesus. They were in desperate need, and they knew that he was the only one who could fulfill their needs. So, they actually searched for Jesus and found him. When they found him, they experienced face-to-face, one-on-one contact, and personal communication with him.

The story of the woman with the issue of blood is found in Matthew 9:20-22, Mark 5:25-34, and Luke 8:43-48. All three writers testified that this woman received her healing from Jesus instantly by touching the edge or hem of his robe (cloak or garment). This woman had been bleeding for twelve years. That is a very long time! She had gone to doctor after doctor, because the Word said doctors, not just one, but, the doctors could not heal her. Then she heard that Jesus was coming through her town. When she got to the place where Jesus was, she found that there were a crowd of people who had already surrounded him. Just like everyone else that was there in the crowd trying to receive something from Jesus, she joined the crowd and pressed her way into it to get to him. This woman had made up her mind to just touch him or his clothes. Her faith was built around what she believed in her heart. She had said to herself that if she could just touch him. If she could just touch some little piece of him, she would be healed or made whole. Through her determination, she pressed through the crowd and got close enough to Jesus to reach in through the people and touch his cloak. It seems obvious that she had to get down, possibly on the ground, in order to reach in and touch his garment, because one translation says that she touched the hem of his garment. The hem indicates that it must have been the bottom of his cloak. In those days, the people cloaks or garments were long. As to whether she was in a crawling, crouching, or lying to be trampled position we do not know, but it can be assumed that she was close to the ground when she touched his cloak.

This woman made a connection and contacted Jesus. By her doing what she did and having a mind that said to her that she would be healed if she touched him, she became whole instantly after the touch. When she made the contact with Jesus, a rush of power went out from his body, and that power transcended into her body. *GLORY TO GOD!* The moment she touched his cloak, she was healed and Jesus knew it. Then he called her forward by asking **"Who touched me (Mark 5:31, NIV)?"** The woman with a grateful but fearful heart came forward from within the crowd, fell at Jesus' feet and told him all about the condition that she had been battling with for twelve long years. Jesus said to her that her faith had healed her. Then he told her to go in peace.

Next, the account of the Canaanite woman also known as the Syrophoenician woman is found in Matthew 15: 21-28 and Mark 7: 24-30. This woman heard that Jesus was in her town or somewhere in the vicinity of her town of Tyre. Jesus was trying to keep a low profile at that time. He did not want anyone to know that he was there. Evidently, he went to someone's house in secret to get away from the crowd that surrounded him everywhere he went. But, this woman found him as soon as she heard that he was there. She had a daughter who was possessed with a demon. The woman came, fell at his feet and begged Jesus to heal her daughter. Jesus' disciples asked him to send her away because her begging bothered them. At first, Jesus said nothing to the woman; then, he told her that he was there to help the lost sheep of Israel and that he needed to help them first. Jesus told her that it was not right to throw or give the children of God's bread to the dogs. The woman answered him and said that even the dogs under the masters' tables eat the crumbs that fall from the tables. Jesus reply to her was that her response to him showed that she had *GREAT FAITH*. Then he said to her that she may go, because the demon had left her daughter. When the woman got home, she found her child lying on the bed completely free of the demon that possessed her.

The disciples asked Jesus to send this woman away, because she continuously cried after them. But, this woman would not be denied access to Jesus, and she would not be denied the thing that she sought after him for. If the disciples told her to go away, she did not, because she did not allow them to intimidate her. She was determined to get what she came for. Jesus saw her boldness, her tenacity and most of all her believing heart. She had faith in him, because she knew that only Jesus could rid her daughter of the demon that tormented her.

The disciples, on the other hand, tried to make her leave; because they knew that she was a gentile, a Greek woman. Their dealings and concerns had been mainly with the Israelites, so they felt no sense of obligation to do anything for her. The disciples probably thought that she really had no real knowledge of Jesus and his purpose on earth. Even Jesus said to her that he came for the lost sheep of Israel, and she did not belong to the sheepfold. He made a comparison to everyone outside of the sheepfold to dogs. But, this woman would not allow herself to be offended by what he said to her. She did not become defensive. She fell at his feet and addressed him as Lord. She knew that she needed his mercy; therefore, her reply to him after being called a dog was that masters do not run the dogs away without them getting at least some crumbs. In essence, this woman was saying that she was asking for very little compared to what Jesus was doing for the Jews. She did not ask to stay there and be counted among the Jews. She did not even ask for salvation. As a matter of fact, she did not ask anything for herself personally. She only asked him to rid her little daughter of the evil spirit that possessed her. Jesus saw her faith and granted her request. She had the kind of faith in him that would not be denied. Jesus called her faith—**Great faith.**

There is a beautiful story about a woman who anointed Jesus with oil from an alabaster jar found in all four of the Gospels: Matthew 26: 6-13; Mark 14: 1-10; Luke 7: 36-50 and John 12:1-11. This is not a story about a miracle that all of a sudden happened to the woman, but a story of worship and appreciation to Jesus; although, it is certain that she had experienced a miraculous encounter with Jesus. While he was in Bethany at Simon, the Leper's home, having dinner with him, this woman came and sat at his feet. In the Book of John she is called Mary. Jesus was being honored at the dinner and several other people were there including Lazarus whom Jesus had raised from the dead and his sister Martha was serving. Many people believe that this particular Mary was Lazarus and Martha's sister, because she was doing what their sister Mary did whenever Jesus was around her— sitting at his feet. Others believe that she was Mary Magdalene whom seven demons had been cast out of, because Simon said in his heart that this was a sinful woman. Simon thoughts were that if Jesus knew about her life, he probably would not want her near him, but Jesus heard his thoughts and spoke to him about them. He told Simon a parable about two people who were in debt and could not pay. One person owed a little money and the other person owed a lot of money. The lender or the person that they were indebted to forgave them and released them from their debts. Then Jesus asked Simon which person he thought would love the moneylender more; Simon replied the one who owed the most money. Then Jesus said to him that he had answered correctly. He further told him that when he came into his house that he did not give him water to wash his feet, but this woman wet his feet with her tears and wiped them with her hair. Simon did not give him a kiss, but Mary from the time that Jesus entered into the house did not stop kissing his feet. Lastly, he told Simon that he did not put oil on his head, but Mary poured perfume oil on his feet. Therefore, her many sins had been forgiven, and she was demonstrating that she loved him much.

This woman loved and appreciated Jesus so much that she anointed him with a very valuable bottle of oil. The fragrant was very pleasant and pleasing, and the aroma filled up the room. The authors said that the disciples called it an expensive jar of perfume which could have been sold for over a year's worth of wages. They questioned and made comments about the act in which she poured the whole jar of oil on Jesus. They felt that she had wasted something that could have been sold for a high price which could have been used to help the poor. Jesus had to tell them to leave the woman alone, because they rebuked her for wasting the oil. He told them that they would have the poor with them always, but they would only have him for a little while longer.

Mary had anointed him for his burial, and it was in line with the will of God. This woman brought the jar of oil with her when she heard that Jesus was in her town. She went there with purpose in her mind to give him perhaps the best gift that she could possible give him. Since this gift represented a large sum of money, Mary presented it to Jesus in appreciation and gratitude to him for what he had done in her life. Because Jesus is the deliverer, he had set her free from the very sinful life that Simon thought about when she touched Jesus. No one knew the liberty and the good feelings that she was experiencing except she and Jesus. With her tears came a cleansing that only Jesus could give, and by the act that she did toward him showed gratefulness that came from deep within. Just being in the presence of Jesus allowed her to get rid of the sins that had her bound. She was cleansed from filthiness and the feelings of shame and guilt. If the woman had taken the time to ask the disciples should she anoint Jesus, they would have said no. If it was left up to man, she would not have gotten near Jesus. But, she did what the Holy Spirit had placed on the inside of her to do. Jesus told the disciples that she has anointed him for his burial, and she would always be remembered for it. When the gospel is preached around the world her story would be told, because he wanted the beauty of deliverance and love shown to the world.

Still there were many other women that God blessed during the time Jesus lived on earth and after he descended up to heaven. In Luke 8:1-3, the Scripture informs us that women traveled with Jesus and his disciples while they went from one town and village to another, proclaiming the good news of the kingdom of God. Mary Magdalene who was delivered from seven demons, Joanna who was the manager of Herod's household, Susanna and many others women that had been delivered from evil spirits and diseases were among the women traveling with them. These women helped to support them out of their own wealth. Martha and Mary, Lazarus' sisters were often found in the company of Jesus. After being in the present of Jesus and spending time with him, who would not tell of his goodness and loving kindness? *That is what preaching the gospel is all about!*

After Jesus was crucified, and his body placed into the tomb, the day after the Sabbath Mary Magdalene, Mary the mother of James, and Salome brought spices to anoint Jesus' body according to Mark 16: 1. All four of the Gospels wrote that the women went to the tomb and were met by an angel, but only one of the Gospels name all three of these women. When they arrived at the tomb, they found that the stone had been rolled away and Jesus' body was no longer there. An angel appeared to them dressed in a white robe and told them not to be alarmed, because Jesus had risen from the dead just as he had told his disciples that he would. The angel told the women to go and tell the disciples that they were to go to Galilee, and Jesus would meet them there. The women were shocked and trembling, but they carried out the assignment that the angel gave them. The disciples did not believe them when they told them. Jesus appeared and spoke to Mary Magdalene personally because she stayed behind weeping. Being the compassionate loving Savior that he is, he spoke to her hurt first when he asked why she was crying. Then he assured her that he was alright and everything was going as it was divinely planned by God.

It was obvious that the women did not abandon him even after his death, for they came to care for his body after his death. Because they were there at the right time in the right place, the angel and Jesus were able to communicate with them and relay a very important message to the disciples first and then to the rest of the world throughout eternity. It was the women who carried the message of the good news that Jesus had risen first. They were given the assignment to go and tell the disciples, and of course I am sure that they told others too.

According to Acts 1: 12-14; 2: 1-18, there were women present at the Pentecost. God gave gifts to sons and daughters to prophesy and preach on that day after the rushing mighty wind came into the room where they were filled with the Holy Spirit. Peter stood up with the twelve disciples and made it very clear to all who were trying to determine whether they were drunk or not because they were speaking in other tongues by quoting the prophet Joel of the Old Testament: **"'In the last days, God says, I will pour out my Spirit on all people. Your sons and daughters will prophesy, your young men will see visions, your old men will dream dreams. Even on my**

servants, both men and women, I will pour out my Spirit in those days, and they will prophesy (Acts 2: 17-18, NIV).'" Peter was telling the people that the prophecy of old had come to pass, and they were seeing it with their own eyes and hearing it with their own ears. The daughters were there, the Holy Spirit was poured on them too, and they were prophesying along with the men. They were also dragged off and put into prison along with the men when the great persecution of the church was going on according to Acts 8:3.

In Acts 9: 36-42, the author called Dorcas, who was the same as Tabitha, a disciple which meant that she followed Jesus' teaching closely and was a dedicated Christian. He described her as someone who was always doing good and helping the poor. She was a maker of fine robes and other clothing, which probably brought in a lot of money. Tabitha became sick and died, and some of the other disciples living near her called for Peter. Peter went into the room where she was laying and prayed for her. She opened her eyes. Then Peter took her by the hand and helped her up on her feet. Then he called the widows and disciples who were there mourning for her and presented her alive to them. This was known throughout their region, and many people believed the Lord.

Chapter 15

Women Ministers that Paul Sanctioned

In Acts 27: 11-15, Paul and his traveling companions went to Philippi, the leading city in the Macedonia district and stayed there several days. On the Sabbath, they went to the river outside of the city gate to find a place of prayer. Some women were gathered there, so they sat down and preached to them. These women had gathered for prayer. Lydia was one of the women listening to Paul's message. She was already a worshipper of God who was also a business woman that dealt in purple cloth from the city of Thyatira. She responded to Paul's message, because the Lord opened her heart. Lydia and her whole household were baptized. Then she invited and persuaded Paul and his traveling companions to stay at her house. Because Lydia accepted the message of Christ and his disciples, the church of Philippi was established. Under Lydia's leadership, through her influence and by her financial and moral support, the church was maintained. In other words, it was a woman who founded and was instrumental in leadership in the Philippians Church that Paul wrote the letter to, which became the Book of Philippians in the New Testament.

Women played very significant roles in establishing the New Testament churches. They were among the men prophesying and operating in the gifts that lifted up the name of Jesus. For example, in Acts 21: 9; the author says that Philip, who was an evangelist, had four unmarried daughters who prophesied. When reading through the rest of the Bible, it is clear that women were used by God in all areas of ministry. Most people especially men who want to be in control and dominate over women love to quote what Paul wrote to the church in I Corinthians 14: 34-35 and to Timothy in I Timothy 2: 11-12. He wrote that the women should be silent and learn in quietness. In I Timothy 2: 12, Paul stated that he do not permit a woman to teach or have authority over a man. It is ironic that Paul, who wrote fourteen books out of twenty-seven books in the New Testament, made these bold statements which men hold to be a law of the church today over women's heads. It's ironic, because the same Paul wrote about many Godly women, such as Priscilla, Lois, Eunice, Euodia, Syntyche, Phoebe, Nympha, and Junias. He recognized these women in some of his other writings as leaders in the body of Christ.

Mark, who was the author of the Book of Acts, wrote about a woman, named Priscilla in Acts 18. This is the same Mark that wrote the Book of Mark. He traveled with and served as Paul's understudy or student. In verses 18 and 19, Mark clearly pointed out that Priscilla traveled with Paul and others. Paul left Priscilla and Aquila at Ephesus. The author further described Priscilla along with Aquila as teachers who had a deeper understanding of the way of God. When people names are mentioned together as a team, it has been often explained to me that the most domain one of the two or more is the leading person. Priscilla's name is first in the twenty-six verse. She and Aquila explained to Apollos the way of God more adequately. In other words she taught Apollos some things; although he was already a very learned man who refuted the Jews in public debates in order to prove that the Scriptures show that Jesus was the Christ. Paul honored her in Romans 16: 3-5 when he wrote to the Roman church. He called her his fellow worker along with Aquila who was her husband. Paul said they risked their lives for him and all of the Gentiles churches which were grateful to them. He asked them to greet Priscilla, Aquila and the church that met at their house. On another occasion in I Corinthians 16: 19,

Paul wrote and this time, he sent greetings from Aquila, Priscilla and the church that was meeting at their house which indicated that he was there with them. Also, in II Timothy 4: 19, Paul asked Timothy to greet them which tells us that Priscilla worked diligently in the ministry of God to get the gospel of Jesus out. She probably won many souls at the expense of risking her own life. But that's what people who are souled out to Christ do. Women sell out to Jesus just as men do; so why shouldn't they be used in every office that men are used in.

Lois and Eunice were highly spoken of by Paul; he gave them the credit for raising Timothy up to be the man of God that he was. Acts 16: 1-3 stated that Timothy's mother was a Jewess and a believer, but his father was a Greek. Timothy was a disciple of Jesus, because his mother and grandmother had brought him up learning the Word and walking in the things of God. Paul wrote two letters to Timothy, because he was Timothy's mentor. Timothy traveled with him and helped to establish and set up many churches. On occasions, Paul left Timothy with some churches to further build doctrines of Christ. In the Book of II Timothy 1: 5, Paul told Timothy that he knew that he had sincere faith, because that sincere faith lived in his grandmother Lois and his mother Eunice. Paul accredited these two women for passing down faithfulness to their offspring who was Timothy. They had trained him well in the things of God, because they themselves lived by the ways of God. Lois and Eunice were role models for Timothy. Children learn what they are taught by looking at others. We just need them to look at the right ones or one (preferably Jesus) and follow the right footsteps.

In the last chapter of the Book of Romans, Paul sent personal greetings to certain people in his letter that he wrote to the saints in Rome. He called them by their names and admonished them for the wonderful works that they had done and was doing for Christ. He began Chapter 16 by asking the saints there to receive Phebe who would be coming to them shortly. He told them to assist her in whatever she needed them to do, because she had helped many people including himself. Paul called her a servant which translates, a deacon of the church in Cenchrea. Evidently, she was going to Rome to work or to service the saints in the ministry. Paul further said that she was worthy of high honor which indicated that she walked in some capacity of leadership and authority as a teacher among the saints. Phebe supported Paul and the work of the church financially. She traveled to other churches and served as a missionary and evangelist.

Paul went on in his letter and asked the readers to greet certain saints. Among the named was Junias; he called her and Andronics, a man, his relatives who had been in prison with him. Paul said, **"They are outstanding among the apostles, and they were in Christ before I was (Romans 16: 7, NIV)."** Here we find a woman called an Apostle by Paul. That's right! I said a woman was named among the apostles. He also asked them to greet Mary, Tryphena, Tryphosa, and Persis who were women that worked hard in the Lord.

In Philippians 4: 2-3, Paul recognized Euodia and Syntyche as women who had worked hard with him as co-workers telling the Good News. In other words, they preached the gospel. He urged the saints there to help them, because their names were written in the Book of Life. Paul relayed the idea that those women were the leaders in the church and that the people needed to help them in making sure that they did not destroy their ministry due to the disagreements between them. The people looked at them as Godly leaders who they could follow into all truths.

In Colossians 4: 15, Paul wrote to the saints in Colosse. Toward the end of the letter, he asked them to greet or to say hello to Nympha and the church in her house. Nympha held a high position in the church in her house. She probably was the main teacher or pastor who had followers. At the end of the letter, Paul wrote to the receiver of the letter to make sure that he read the letter in the church of the Laodiceans. Finally, he said that he had written the letter in his own handwriting. So, Paul acknowledged many women as teachers of the Good News in the body of Christ. Most of the women that he acknowledged in his letters to the different towns and churches were spoken of as equals to him in the hard work that they did and were doing in the ministry of Jesus Christ. So, as for the letters that Paul wrote to the Corinthians and to Timothy about women not being allowed to teach and having no authority over a man, it must have been for that particular church at that particular time; that is the belief that Bible scholars teach anyway. Paul wrote in **Galatians 3: 28: "There is neither Jew nor Greek, slave nor free, male nor female, for you are all one in Christ Jesus (NIV)."** If Paul once believed that women should not teach or have authority over a man, somewhere he misquoted himself, because he told men in other places and during other times to receive certain women in the ministry.

Chapter 16

Conclusion

God, who is the author and the finisher of our faith and fate, made sure that the Bible included women who worked hard for Him. He also made it very clear that women are very important to Him and that their callings have nothing to do with man initially. Their callings are all about God and them, because we all were created with a purpose from God, not man. When God created the woman, He made a specific, special person and set her aside for his use. It was God that made her and gave her purpose and destiny not man. Man cannot fulfill a woman's assignment from God nor can a woman fulfill a man's assignment from God; therefore, everyone needs to be aware and practice doing what God told them to do and stop blocking the assignments of the woman given by God. Because God is the Creator, and He is not a respecter of person, He can use and has used whomever He wants, whenever He wants, and in what area He wants. No man knows the heart and mind of God, because He said that his thoughts and His ways are so much higher than man's (our) thoughts and ways.

By singling out each of the women that I have written about in this book, it is my hope and desire that you, the reader, have gained some insight of God's love, compassionate, and care for women. It is also my hope that you saw the heart and determination of the women to fulfill the assignments that God gave them to do. I believe that these women showed that they were the ones to get the jobs done that God needed to be done. After all, God Himself hand-picked them for specific purposes. Not only did He hand-pick them, He also sent an angel with the message straight from Him (God) as to what they were to do. You saw during several divine meetings, God did not send the angel to a man first, He sent him directly to the woman. OUR GOD IS AWESOME! The Word of God tells us that God changes not. He is the same today, yesterday and forever. And since we are people of faith who believe the Word of God, then we should understand and know that He still uses men and women however He chooses to use them. It is not man or woman's calling, gifting or ministry to tell anyone who they are in God or what they should be doing in ministry. Men and women can only bear witness to what God has already told the person or their parents first who he/she is or who he/she was created to be.

We, women have had to suffer many unnecessary things from the hands of men and other women who cannot discern the mind and heart of God. Not realizing that they have allowed themselves to be used by Satan, some people in ministry spend a lot of time abusing women in ministry emotionally which can be considered to be physical abuse too. Because after one has been emotionally abused for so long, it takes a toll on one physical health and visa-versa. You cannot have one without the other, because they go together.

Several years ago, I heard an apostle make the statement that a pastor is married to the church and that their wives should learn to live with it. That statement cannot be any further from the truth, because the Bible says that the bride of Christ is the church. So, if the pastor is married to the church, then he has taken Christ's bride. The Bible says that the church is being prepared to be Christ's bride without spots or wrinkles. Everyone in today's church will not make it to the marriage as brides, because with the help of Christ, the church is making itself pure, holy, and acceptable to be His bride. Some people do not seek God at all. They don't want His help, and they sure are not trying to make themselves pure without spots of wrinkles. They love being backstabbers, talebearers, slanderers, and gossipers. These people in the church are not even interested in becoming His bride. All they are interested in is becoming somebody big in church with a title, and they do not care who they hurt to get there. Most of the time, they used their money and/or influence with others to get some type of position in church. Evidently, some pastors live by this idea too and accept brides from wicked people, because they make their wives secondary to the church (the people). Their wives end up being subjected and abused by them (their husbands) and the church members. That sounds like and feels like spiritual adultery to me which in most cases end up in natural adultery, because pastors who are husbands feel that they should give more of their time to the church (certain individuals) which leave very little or no time for their wives and children.

Also, a pastor is to shepherd the sheep or act as a father to the church members. So, to say that he is married to the church makes him someone who is committing incest with his children. That sounds very sick, but in many cases, it holds to be true. These beliefs, attitudes and practices are becoming more and more wide-spread; therefore, more pastors' marriages are ending up in divorce. The church in this case and in many cases plays the harlot that is there to destroy the pastor's marriage and family. Satan has waged war against the body of Christ, and he has twisted the Word of God to deceive man once again. Sadly, enough it is working, because in order to do the most damage to the body of Christ, he starts with the head first. Men's in the five-fold ministry marriages are failing all over the world, and when they allow themselves to fail at their own marriages, people look at them with a sense of disbelief. It has become an epidemic, and I am sure Satan is enjoying it. **But there is a remnant of people that will get to be Christ's bride.**

Not only are women, pastors' wives especially, being abused because of incorrect teachings about the role that a church, actually the members, is supposed to play in the pastors' lives, they are also being abused due to jealousy from their husbands, church members and other so called believers. Because men have this ego issue going on in their heads, they cannot stand it when their wives are used mightily by God. I have seen and continue to see this scenario over and over again. A lot of the time, they proudly take credit for work that their wives and/or other women do. Men love to be praised, and they think more highly of themselves than they ought to, like Naabal and Saul, the king did. You have heard the saying, 'behind every good man is a good woman.' It is a true saying in a lot of cases whether the men are married or single, because even the single men have women handling their business. The women are usually the ones that provide the ideas in order for the program to go over well. If the women do not think of the idea, then they are certainly the ones that do most of the labor to bring it into existence. To be clear and fair, the saying does not apply to all men. Some men are very smart and industrious, and they do what they need to do to accomplish their dreams and goals with the help of women or other men.

Men use the Scripture to their advantage in order to lord over and control women. This goes all the way back to Genesis where God told Eve that her desires will be toward her husband and that he will rule over her. They also refer to New Testament Scriptures that says the man is head of the woman and a woman is not allowed to have authority over a man in the church. But, I have addressed these Scriptures in this book, and I hope that I have put them in context for you. I am sure that Paul never thought for one minute that these Scriptures would be used to antagonize and hold women captive under man's rule. After all, if you recall it was Paul who told men in certain towns and cities to receive some women and honor them as ministers in the gospel. Also, it was Paul that told men to love their wives as they did their own body, and see to it that they did not mistreat their wives.

Men and women display jealous attitudes toward women in ministry, on a wide-spread but mainly toward pastor's wives. I have yet to meet a pastor's wife who can testify that she has not ever experienced negative behaviors, such as jealousy and slander against her in the church. Today, most of them say that their husband, the pastor, has led or leads the pack of slanderers against them. People, men and women desire to be the pastor's help-meet. They want to be his right-hand man or woman, but Scriptural, that is the place that his wife holds. So, they all go through these stages of confusion which Satan uses to create division and havoc in the church which leads to a broken home and a broken church. The process is simple, and it is the same tactic that Satan used in the Garden of Eden on Adam and Eve. Satan's plan was to come between God and man's perfect peaceful relationship. His plan is used all over the world in many battles; it is called Divide and Conquer. Satan, through the mouths of members of the church, flatters the pastor just like the serpent did Eve. They tell him how good and how great he is. These church people use the name of God a lot to help justify their flattery toward him, until they make him feel that he is the one single most important person that the church functions through and without him the church would fail. In other words, they make him feel as though he is a king sitting on the throne in the church. Then they begin to point out things to him about his wife that makes her look like she is against him especially if she tries to advise him in righteousness toward them. God is the only supreme King of the church. To the Pastors' wives who are reading this book, does this sound familiar to you? After they have planted enough seed or a better description would be enough discontentments in his head against his wife, he begins to believe that he is mighty all by himself and that he has to prove it. I have seen some very cold-hearted evil-spirited pastors do mean things to their wives and children, and I have experienced some of it myself. Pastors treat their wives as if they were their number one enemy just because of what church members have said to them about their wives. These situations become a vicious cycle of abuse to the pastor's wives and in some cases have applied to other women in ministry that people are jealous of. Through ignorant and greed, church members have come between many pastors and their wives. They do not think twice about being instrumental in destroying families and ministries, because they are Satan's children calling themselves God's children in the church. Most of the times, since the other women who are ministers are not bound by being married to the pastor, they move on to another church, one that would let them operate in their calling from God. But, sadly enough, the pastor's wife is stuck there to be abused even more. Her only options are to stay and pray hard that her husband will wake up from his stupor and repent or get out.

From the beginning and all throughout the Bible, God used women to bring their sons and daughters into the world. Of course, He is still using women to do so. God had His messenger angels to speak specifically to mothers and fathers about their children. In several incidents, the angel only spoke to the women, because it is the mother's responsibility to teach her children at home. In other words, she should be the one who is closest to her child and who is speaking the most in his life which shapes and trains him into who is to become. In today's church, members of the church have become such a sore in the pastor's family and others ministers' family that our children are suffering beyond repair. There is a lot of talk bad mouthing the preacher's kids (PK's), and you can already guess that the talk or slander is coming from the church members. They think that they are in the church to watch and correct the preacher's wife and children. They spend so much time putting expectations on the preacher's children until they forget to put any on their own children. They certainly do not correct their children when they should. The preacher's children are looked at and regarded as someone who should act perfect instead of acting like normal children. They are treated like Ismael and Hagar treated Isaac because of who they are. Sadly enough, this is another crucial area of frustration for the pastor's wife. She sees what is being done to her children due to envy, jealousy and ignorance, but she does not have the kind of husband that Sarah had. Because Abraham was a man that sought God, God directed his footsteps and decisions. God caused him to send the source of their problems away; therefore, Sarah and Isaac were able to live in peace, joy and happiness in the LORD. Today, the pastor feels that he needs the church members more than he needs his family. Sadly, most preachers' kids experience so much hurt and abuse from church members that they end up hating church. They are targeted by the members and their fathers cater to the members most of the time.

We often see the trend and also teach the principle that an apple tree produces apple trees. In the Bible, men trained their sons and daughters to do what they did occupational wise. God named a specific tribe or family to be the priests and ministers in His temple. The first priest placed in office by God was Aaron, and his sons were priests also. They were in the same immediately family and blood line. Priests produced priests, but doctors produce doctors. Children whose parents practice certain professions are happy to become what they have grown-up seeing their parents do. Because that is what they are familiar with, they already have knowledge of the occupation and training in it. But, preachers' kids are not running to college to be a pastor or any other kind of minister. Most of them can hardly wait to get from under their parents, so they don't have to do anything that has to deal with church members. Now, we can see that Satan has executed a plan against the preachers' kids that is working in his favor, because the world has been and is being cheated out of the young apostles, prophets, evangelists, pastors, and teachers that our children were supposed to become.

It is my prayer that God will call all men and women in ministry that are walking in error to repentance so that they can reunite with God and their family and walk in righteousness. Then once again, they can become someone the people can look up to and be taught by, because when men do not respect their wives and treat their children right, then people do not respect them. How can people respect them when most importantly, their own family cannot respect them? Satan has conquered them, and they may as well be having church with Satan as their God, because Satan is who they are displaying and honoring.

As a senior pastor and a divorce woman who experienced emotional and spiritual abuse from the pastor and church members, it would be only fitting to tell any woman or man that just because your spouse let the devil use him or her that does not mean that you give up on God. Paul said it this way, **"But if the unbeliever leaves, let him do so. A believing man or woman is not bound in such circumstances; God has called us to live in peace. Nevertheless, each one should retain the place in life that the Lord assigned to him to which God has called him (I Corinthians 7: 15 & 17, NIV)."** In other words, men and women of God, your ministry was assigned to you by the Lord not by man or the attachment that you may have to a certain man or a certain woman. My apostle said to me that God still expects me to do what He called me to do, and my circumstances did not change that fact. My assignment was not given to me just because I was some man's wife; it was given to me because God created me to be who I am, and my creation came with an assignment from God. So, I have to complete my assignment in order to be fulfilled. I love being a pastor which allows me to feed (to teach) the Lord Jesus' sheep.

This book is written to inspire every woman in ministry who has been discouraged and persuaded that certain callings in ministry really isn't for them to do simply because they are women. If you seek God first and his righteousness, then most likely, ministry is for you, because God is not in the business of using just any old body with any old kind of life style. He certainly does not use people just because they are men, who feel they should be the head in the church; God uses everyone. The biggest problem in the church today is that everyone does not know what their place is, and most people are out of order which is causing confusion and division. The reason the pastor's wife has been singled out in this book is because she is in most cases the number one person victimized with this kind of mistreatment and abuse. She makes all kinds of sacrifices for the work of the ministry without receiving the credit or the honor that she deserves. In many cases, at the end, she is pushed out of or shut down in the church affairs, and in some cases she is put out of the church altogether where she worked so hard to help build and establish. Everyone has a specific place in the body of Christ, and no one can define your place. God is the only one that can do that, and chances are He is not talking to everyone else about you. He talks to you personally about your calling. So, it is your responsibility to know why God made you, and it is your duty to do what he made you to do. *Selah!*

It is also my hope that this book does not make men seem that they are all wrong and on their way to hell, because that is not the case nor is it the purpose of this book. Not all men lord over their wives or hold the beliefs that they are superior to women and that women should be under them. But, this belief is not only in the religious community, it is practiced in all areas of our society. The work force treat women inferior to men by paying women less for the same job that men are doing. They also give men the top positions on the job. Women have been fighting for equal rights for a long time, although it has gotten better, the equal rights for women have a long way to go to reach equality. Nevertheless, there are many God fearing Spirit-filled men who are walking in righteousness. There are many men in ministry that are living right, hopefully more men than not living right. There are many apostles, prophets, evangelists, pastors, and teachers that are good righteous role models, and we are thankful to God for these true men of God. But for the men who are walking in error, I pray that after reading this book, they will seek God for His wisdom and understanding. Then when they see God as Isaiah did, they will see themselves, because every solider that God has need to be in his place so he and God can get victory in the battle against Satan. But as long as men and women that are supposed to be on God side keep letting Satan use them, then we cannot be victorious.

I hope this book will inspire men and women everywhere to examine themselves and their situations and to seek God for their purpose. After learning their purpose, my prayer is that they will fulfill what God has created them to do, because God is not concern about our circumstances. If each individual focus on his or her own calling, then he or she would not have time to mess up someone else's calling. Circumstances and situations are just obstacles put in the way for us to get pass. They can be good or bad, and most certainly most of the time they can be people; as a matter of fact, 99% of the obstacles are people, which are always a hindrance put in the way to keep us from fulfilling our calling from God. They play their roles well, but if we know who we are and whom we are, then we can get pass them. When we realize that they are carrying out Satan's strategies against us, then we will know that they are our tests that are turning into our testimonies; our messes that are turning into our messages, and our war zones that will make our victories even greater. So, I say to every man and every woman the following: answer the call that God has given you, because He is still looking for a man and a woman who will be a willing obedient servant and a solider in His army. If you are willing and obedient, then you are highly favored by the Lord, and you will eat the fat of the land.

Also, to every reader of this book—if this book has encouraged you or blessed you in any way, then pass it on to others that you know who need to be encouraged and blessed. Every woman in ministry should read this book and be ministered to. Every man of God should be familiar with the contents of this book. So, even if this book does not minister to you, perhaps you know someone that it will minister to. I urge you to buy it and give it as a gift to encourage someone who is in need of a Rhema Word from God.